Criminal Justice
Recent Scholarship

Edited by
Marilyn McShane and Frank P. Williams III

A Series from LFB Scholarly

Narcissism and Entitlement
Sexual Aggression and the College Male

David R. Champion

LFB Scholarly Publishing LLC
New York 2003

Library of Congress Cataloging-in-Publication Data

Champion, David R.
  Narcissism and entitlement : sexual aggression and the college male /
David R. Champion.
      p. cm. -- (Criminal justice)
Includes bibliographical references and index.
  ISBN 1-931202-49-4
  1. Sexual animosity. 2. Entitlement attitudes. 3. Narcissism. 4.
Male college students--United States--Psychology. I. Title. II.
Criminal justice (LFB Scholarly Publishing LLC)
  BF692.15 .C47 2002
  306.7'081--dc21

2002010689

ISBN 1-931202-49-4

Printed on acid-free 250-year-life paper.

Manufactured in the United States of America.

Table of Contents

v

Acknowledgements

I would like to gratefully acknowledge my committee members for their guidance, assistance and support in the completion of this project. In particular, I am grateful to Dr. Randy Martin for his hard work, suggestions and encouragement. Dr. Dennis Giever, Dr. Alida Merlo and Dr. Donald Robertson were also of invaluable assistance.

Furthermore, I am grateful to Jonas   Cavileer and Kyle Green for their assistance in the data collection process. Thanks also to Dennis Siepierski for his invaluable technical expertise and limitless patience.

In addition, I am grateful to my parents, William and Martha Champion, for their support, wisdom and faith. I am very thankful for the love, faith and support of Janice, whose patience and suggestions were of great help to me in my doctoral work. Finally, I wish to thank Ian and Jake for their important support and assistance.

Preface

This study sought to identify cognitively structured belief systems of men that are associated with sexual aggression. The structures of narcissism and Machiavellianism were tested among other variables in order to determine if certain entitling belief systems had a relationship with sexual violence.

Established instruments that measured narcissism, Machiavellianism and sexual aggression were administered to a sample of 308 male students. The subjects were also asked if they participated in collegiate athletics or fraternities, as well as their ages, sexual experience and number of credits earned in college. The results were analyzed via descriptive statistics, comparison of means, correlations, and regression. These results indicated that high sexual aggressors tended to be high in narcissism, Machiavellianism and sexual experience. Age was also positively correlated with sexual aggression. However, these variables did not contribute or explain sexual aggression, they were merely associated with it. The other variables were unrelated to sexual aggression.

This study indicates that certain personality structures might be associated with sexual aggression, and that these should be further investigated to develop a greater understanding of the causes of this criminal activity. Men who report high sexual experience may also tend to be more sexually aggressive because of their self-serving cognitions.

Entitlement and self-servingness are not novel approaches to understanding criminal behavior. Certainly, these are intuitive and popular notions of how criminals think and behave, among laypersons and scholars alike. Pervasive syllogisms such as "that guy thinks he's God's gift to women," or even the (hopefully) tongue-in-cheek statement that "it's all about me!" hint at the understanding that inflated self-regard seems to underlie behavior that is at the least obnoxious, if not predatory.

This work attempted to rework this understanding into a measurable model of entitlement. Besides excessive self-regard, the model incorporated related Machiavellian correlates such as manipulativeness, deceitfulness, low conventional morality and other antisocial tendencies into the entitlement framework. It was premised that an entitled individual might also be more likely to be sexually acquisitive, so participants were asked to estimate their sexual experience in relation to their peers. Finally, other individual variables that attempted to tap into rape-supportive peer culture were embedded into the concept: namely, athletic participation and fraternity membership.

The results were somewhat interesting, with empirical support for some parts of the model but not for others. The results lend support to the notion of an entitlement model as a viable framework against which to impose certain types of criminal behaviors, given further development and research.

CHAPTER 1

Sexual Aggression as a Problem

INTRODUCTION

Rape and other forms of sexual violence leave enduring, devastating effects on the victims. Dunn, Vail-Smith and Knight (1999) described rape as a "traumatic, life-altering experience" (p. 213). Research has demonstrated that rape victims suffer from lingering feelings of excessive vulnerability, agoraphobia, and sexual anxieties (Resick, Veronen, Kilpatrick, Calhoun, & Atkeson, 1986; Mayer & Ottens, 1994). Lansky (1995) presented case evidence of victim nightmares that extend beyond the sexual violence itself to feelings of shame, guilt and fragility. Frank, Anderson, Stewart, Dancu and West (1988) reported that along with nightmares, sexual assault victims also suffer from major depression, increased suspicion, somatic symptoms, and problems with social functioning (as cited in Mayer & Ottens, 1994).

Other researchers have also identified long-term effects of sexual violence on victims. Calhoun, Atkeson, and Resick (1982) identified chronic fear reactions among rape survivors. Burgess and Holmstrom (1985) purported that rape victims suffer from a variety of enduring, debilitating effects they labeled as "Rape Trauma Syndrome" (RTS). Among the symptoms of RTS are guilt, numbness, hyper-alertness, difficulties in sleeping, memory/concentration impairment, and re-living the trauma.

Although the traumatic effects of sexual violence are well documented, the causes of this aggression remain unclear. Most research indicates that sexual violence is driven by a combination of variables. While social and behavioral scientists investigate the causes of sexual violence, official statistics recount the reported instances of rape and sexual crimes. However, the true prevalence of the problem remains largely unknown. It is equally clear that rape is not the only form of sexual aggression with which society should be concerned. Unwanted fondling, touching, and verbal innuendoes and leers all represent varying degrees of aggressive behavior.

While policy, legislation, and their enforcement are all important responses to the problem of sexual coercion, it is also necessary to investigate the underlying causes of sexual violence. Further research into the causes of sexual aggression will benefit not only the theoretical body of knowledge, but could point to new directions in preventing further violence.

Prevalence of the Problem

The 1999 Uniform Crime Report (UCR) reflected an 8% drop in rape and sexual assaults from 1998, with a reported 193,423 incidents of forcible rape (Federal Bureau of Investigation, Department of Justice). Despite the decrease, there is little reason for optimism, given the low reporting rate of the UCR as evidenced by comparison with the victimization surveys recorded by the Bureau of Justice Statistics (BJS) National Crime Victimization Survey (NCVS).

The NCVS samples households to gather data from crime victims, while the UCR reflects incidents reported to law enforcement. The 1995 NCVS reported nearly 355,000 rape/sexual assaults while less than 125,000 were reported by the UCR for the same time period. The discrepancy of approximately 230,000 incidents between these two sources is typical of the under-reporting of rape and sexual violence to police agencies. In fact, a comparison between the two reporting agencies demonstrates that rape is the most under-reported of violent crimes.

Another salient issue is the fact that studies of rape and other forms of sexual aggression are not evenly distributed, either across age groups or across settings. Many of the studies reported in the rape literature, particularly research that explores multidimensional models of sexual violence, have used university undergraduate males as respondents. While this might be due in part to the convenience of employing such a sample, it can also be argued that campus settings provide a reasonable and appropriate subject pool for this type of research. Overall, university students are young, interact in a variety of social settings, and have reasonably diverse backgrounds. It is primarily young males who commit acts of sexual violence; therefore, it is sensible to sample from a setting where there are a lot of young men. Additionally, many of the social factors associated with rape (such as alcohol consumption and attitudinal cultures that are supportive of the subjugation of women) are part of campus life (Boeringer, Shehan & Akers, 1991; Koss & Oros, 1982; Rapaport & Burkhart, 1984; Schwartz & DeKeseredy, 1998).

Whether sexual violence occurs on or off campus, however, it is always underreported. Discrepancies among the reporting sources (Uniform Crime Report, Federal Bureau of Investigation, 1998; Cusimano & Perkovich, July 6, 2000) accentuate the need to research the problem of sexual aggression. This is especially so when considering that any figures that are available most likely represent only a fraction of the actual occurrences.

In a study of a national sample of college men, Malamuth, Sockloskie, Koss, & Tanaka (1991) tested a model of the aggressive male. The substance of this study will be discussed in Chapter 2. However, in preliminary discussion the authors reported that between 15% and 25% of college men engaged in "some level of sexual aggression" (Malamuth et al., 1991, p. 670). Similarly, approximately 30% of all college students report at least one instance of physical coercion (sexual or otherwise) within a dating relationship, as victims, perpetrators or both (Sugarman & Hotaling, 1989; as cited in Malamuth et al., 1991).

Other studies point to the prevalence of acquaintance rape. Dunn et al. (1999) found that approximately one third of respondents reported knowing one or more victims of date/acquaintance rape. These authors also reported that 80% of all rapes on college campuses were date or acquaintance assaults. Furthermore, they declared that, typically, six to seven female students out of 50 reported victimization by date rapists within the preceding year (Finn, 1995). Rubenzahl (1998) noted that 15%-25% of female college students reported that they were victims of date or acquaintance rape, while 4% to 15% of male students reported that they perpetrated such sexual violence. Koss, Gidycz, and

Wisniewski (1987) reported that 15.4% of college women reported being raped since the age of 14, and 12.1% reported being victimized by an attempted rape. In addition, 11.9% reported being subjected to some form of sexual coercion (Koss et al., 1987). These startling statistics have led researchers to conclude that the prevalence of date/acquaintance rape is "disturbing" (McCaw & Senn, 1998, p. 609) and "pervasive" (Yescavage, 1999, p. 796).

If these findings are accurate, the rates of sexual violence are far higher than indicated by any official reporting agency. It is important, then, to not only investigate the "true" prevalence of sexual violence, but to continue to research theoretical dimensions of sexual aggression. Only through continued research will the social science disciplines be able to develop an understanding into the nature of sexual violence and eventually provide applicable findings for law enforcement, policy makers, educators and treatment providers. As Burgess (1985) wrote, "with the increasing statistics on rape and sexual assault, this is not a private syndrome. It is a public concern and its treatment, from hospital, police and criminal justice-level staff has been addressed...as a public charge" (p. 56).

Defining Rape

Before continuing, it is necessary to define rape, for the purposes of the current study. The definition to be employed draws from Ellis's (1989) conceptualization of rape as "a collection of behavior patterns involving forceful attempts at sexual intimacy" (p. 2). Like Ellis, this work does not restrict itself to the legal statutes that define rape but adopts a more inclusive interpretation. The terms *sexual aggression*, *sexual violence* or *sexual coercion* are used in this study to reflect the premise that rape exists within a continuum of these behaviors, and includes instances of verbal or chemical coercion (such as plying a woman with alcohol or drugs) for the purposes of attaining sexual gratification.

It should also be noted that for the purposes of this study, only adult male victimization of adult females are considered. While it is acknowledged that homosexual rape, pedophilia, and the sexually violent practices of female victimizers are important issues that merit research, these behaviors fall outside the scope of this research. This study is restricted to investigating adult male on adult female sexual violence.

The conceptual interpretation of rape described above is necessary for this study, given the premise that rape might be explained by attitudinal/belief structures (detailed in Chapter 3) and measured by a behavioral continuum scale (also discussed in Chapter 3). This study addresses rape as a behavior that occurs on a continuum of sexual aggression, and not as an act that may or may not be bound by statutory considerations. Legal distinctions are discrete in nature, with specific criteria that must be met to distinguish between indecent assault, sexual battery, sexual harassment, rape and so on. Instead, this work views sexual violence as an act of human aggression that exists on a continuum, to be examined from a cognitive-behavioral standpoint. For the purposes of the current study then, it is inappropriate to define the term *rape* so narrowly.

The Theoretical Context of this Study

Because of the general under-reporting of crimes of sexual aggression, as well as the varying figures reported in the research, it is difficult to assess the true prevalence of sexual violence, whether it occurs on or off campus. However, all of the self-report data indicate what might legitimately be considered as disturbing levels. Considering the harmful effects of sexual violence on its victims, investigation of this problem needs to be continued from a variety of perspectives. This study proposes a theoretical stance that seeks to examine specific attitudinal/personality dimensions of the sexual aggressor.

Research into the sexually aggressive male has diverged into multiple models. Koss and Oros (1982) and Brownmiller (1975) suggested that much of the earlier, traditional investigation of the subject had been based on a typological approach. That is, the rapist has been labeled as an extreme entity within society, whose values and attitudes bear little resemblance to those of the mainstream. The aforementioned authors disputed this model, and proposed a non-typological perception of rape, one that views sexual violence as rooted in and implicitly condoned by society (Koss, 1997). It was argued that it is inappropriate to investigate sexual violence as an outlying behavioral extreme. Sexual aggressors are inhabitants of a societal spectrum, a spectrum that reflects modern culture. The roots of sexual aggression are embedded in society (Koss, 1997). Similarly, Koss and

Oros (1982), as well as Scully (1990) asserted that men might be thought of as occupying a position along a continuum of varying sexually aggressive behavior. According to these authors, some males are more likely to commit acts of sexual violence than are others, but all reside along the same continuum.

Scully (1990) wrote that rape and sexual assault were "discovered" (p. 33) as crimes in the 1970s as a result of heightened media attention, increasing pressure from women's advocacy groups, and a growing volume of scholarly and popular literature on the subject. While rape may have finally been identified as a social problem, it remains, according to Scully, a "women's problem" (p. 34). That is, Scully maintains that mainstream culture continues to ignore the harmful ramifications of rape and sexual violence against women. This seems especially true when the instances of sexual aggression that fall short of the legal definition of rape are considered.

Investigation into sexual aggression has been pursued from a variety of models. Social scientists have conceived of sexual aggression as stemming from medical, psychopathological, anthropological and evolutionary perspectives (Scully, 1990). Scully joined Koss and Oros (1982) in pointing out that all of these approaches were limited, in that only the extreme cases of sexual aggression were measured (that is, the rapists). Koss and Oros proposed that while rape is the profound manifestation of sexual aggression, it is only one conduct among many, dwelling at the far end of a continuum that also contains socially accepted, common behavior. Koss and Oros (1982) conceptualized rape as the endpoint of a range of culturally condoned activities in which males engage to obtain sexual intercourse, a range that also includes verbal pressure and deceit.

Taking the dimensional approach to rape set forth by Koss and Oros (1982), one might view the sexually aggressive male as possessing many of the same personality characteristics as the non-aggressor. The act of rape might then be a result of maladaptive extremes in certain personality attributes of the aggressor, not the mere presence of the characteristics in an individual. In other words, it is the magnitude of aggressor attributes that determine where the individual falls on the continuum, not whether he (this work is about male aggressors only) merely possesses such personality characteristics or not. The current study will employ this dimensional model in attempting to understand the causes of rape and sexual violence.

Relating this to the continuum, non-extreme model discussed in the preceding paragraph, it is only the extreme cases that gain attention (such as an overt act of rape) while lesser magnitudes of that particular personality dimension might exist and be manifested in lesser acts of sexual intimidation (such as brief fondling or verbally aggressive innuendoes).

This dimensional approach is not new to the study of sexual aggression. It has been tested in previous studies measuring various attitudinal scales against sexually assaultive/coercive behaviors (Malamuth, Heavey & Linz 1993; Malamuth, Sockloskie, Koss & Tanaka, 1991; Rapaport & Burkhart, 1984; Schwartz & Nogrady, 1996). These and other studies are further explored in the literature review section of this work.

Research on the dimensional model has examined the roles of various attitudinal variables (including dominance motive, acceptance of interpersonal violence, hostility toward women, and others) and their relationships to sexual aggression. However, there are two belief structures that appear to have relevance to sexually violent behavior, but have received insufficient attention in the literature: Machiavellianism and narcissism.

Both Machiavellianism and narcissism are personality dimensions that enjoy widespread acceptance and use in the social psychological literature. Both are measurable by scales with established reliability and validity (this will be further detailed in Chapter 5). Both explore belief structures with specific items pertaining to how a respondent perceives oneself and others.

Furthermore, it will be argued in Chapter 4 that Machiavellianism and narcissism provide the groundwork for conceptualizing a new theoretical personality construct, one that might help to explain not only rape and sexual assault, but potentially other types of crime as well. That construct is called entitlement.

The Nature of this Work: Criminal Entitlement

The overall stance of this work reflects only an initial step in constructing a model of entitlement that might provide greater understanding and prediction of criminal behavior. Entitlement as a component of sexual aggression and other antisocial activity is an intuitive and popular notion. Focus on this construct as a component of criminal behavior is not new. The criteria of narcissism and psychopathy, as well as the criminal personality models advanced by scholars such as Yochelson and Samenow (1976) and Walters and White (1989) all include some variation of privilege and entitlement as criminal or antisocial characteristics.

However, these popular and intuitive notions of privilege have yet to be organized into a model that links entitling beliefs with their functions. To state that rapists (or indeed any criminals) commit their crimes "because they feel entitled to" may rightly be criticized as both superficial and tautological. Although a readily graspable notion, the proposal that criminals feel privileged and victimize others out of a sense of righteous, rationalized entitlement should be further examined to determine its importance in understanding antisocial and criminal behavior. How do they interact with other psychological constructs to produce criminal behavior? This work attempts to address that issue. Developing this characteristic as a viable blueprint of a sexual coercion model requires further investigation into how these beliefs are sustained, if they are predictably criminogenic across situations, and how they are influenced by social factors. This work is a step in that direction, an initial empirical venture into some of the struts of the model.

To that end, it was necessary to first identify established personality measures that hold theoretical linkages to what might be considered as an entitlement construct. The measures of Machiavellianism and narcissism were selected for three reasons:

> (1) Their combined criteria closely match what the foundation of a criminal entitlement construct would look like: self-servingness, cruelty, devaluation of others, manipulativeness, superiority, lack of empathy, deceitfulness, and other antisocial elements;
> (2) they are well-established in the literature as viable and useful constructs; and
> (3) they are measurable with instruments that have demonstrated reliability and validity.

The functions of these dimensions are discussed in Chapter 2 against a template of cognitive styles and narrative construction. It is premised, *a priori*, that these cognitive frameworks provide a mechanism for the development and activity of entitled thinking. What exactly does this mean? An example might help summarize and clarify this idea.

An "entitled" male may have constructed a symbolically meaningful, mythically derived concept of himself as a lone, heroic figure to whom women are desperately attracted. This man is not delusional; he is not subscribing to a literal belief in a fantasy, he is merely indulging in a cognitive script that underlies his particular uniqueness. In this narrative-cognitive stance, he meets a woman at a party. Driven by self-interest and the sense that he is a figure of importance within a "story," he aggressively pursues her with whatever charm and verbal skills he possesses. She is not interested and tells him so. This jarring discord between his self-sense and the reality of her rejection is the mechanism by which the narcissistic, Machiavellian, entitled dimensions then might lead to intimidating, coercive or assaultive behavior.

Note that it is not proposed that the mere presence of the personality dimensions will lead to the attack, but instead that the interaction of all of the components might account for sexual aggression. However, before this model is developed or researched further, it is imperative to initially test the rigor of some its basic assumptions.

What this Study Does

This study investigates the roles of Machiavellianism and narcissism in sexual aggression among male undergraduate students at a mid-sized university in the northeast. This study examines the theoretical linkages between the more traditional concepts of Machiavellianism and narcissism and what shall be introduced as the emerging concept of entitlement. The theoretical review will be based on social psychological literature that introduces the role of cognitions in the formation of belief structures, specifically Machiavellianism and narcissism. The final section of the literature review will establish conceptual linkages among Machiavellianism, narcissism and entitlement, and will posit that these concepts are positively correlated with sexual aggression.

This work will sample male undergraduate students and administer established scales for Machiavellianism, narcissism and sexual aggression (the dependent variable). Regression analysis was employed to determine the relative impact of Machiavellianism and narcissism in explaining the variance in sexual aggression. Comparison of means was also used to determine the significance of difference in mean scores between high and low Machs and narcissists.

Additionally, this work will investigate other correlates of sexual aggression, derived from the literature, to gain a better understanding of their contributory role, and to provide control variables for the analysis. Questions pertaining to demographic and background information will be added to the scale items. It was anticipated that these correlating items provide data about personal characteristics not covered by the administered scales. Specifically, membership in fraternities, participation in organized athletics, past sexual experience and ages in years of the participants are all variables that have been researched in the past as correlates of sexual aggression, with varying results. The first two variables in particular have been the subject of great interest in criminological scholarship as well as enjoying a certain anecdotal popularity among laypersons. These data may still contribute to a deeper understanding of sexual aggression, and are worth re-exploring, especially as they relate to and interact with the personality dimensions in question.

The current study will examine the following questions that relate to the Machiavellian and narcissism models, and what they might contribute to the dimensional perspective of sexual aggression among males. The concept of entitlement will not be directly tested here, as this is a new conceptual construct for which no scale currently exists. Entitlement will be identified, developed and explored in this work as a theoretical construct. Further investigation into entitlement and the construction of a corresponding scale are venues for later inquiry.

Research Questions

> 1. Are Machiavellianism and narcissism among males correlated with each other?
> 2. Is there an association between Machiavellianism and sexual aggression among males?
> 3. Is there an association between narcissism and sexual aggression among males?
> 4. Are there other personal or demographic variables that are associated with sexual aggression among males?

The second chapter will outline the aspects of social/cognitive psychology literature that are relevant to the understanding of how personality dimensions may influence sexually aggressive behavior. Chapter 3 reviews literature on sexual violence and Chapter 4 discusses how this behavior is related to Machiavellianism, narcissism and aggression. The final section of this theoretical overview will introduce the belief structure of entitlement. It will be argued that entitlement may be derived from the established constructs of narcissism and Machiavellianism, and is based on the social psychological groundwork established in Chapter 2.

Chapter 5 will propose the methodology of this study, and will cover issues of sampling, instruments, reliability and validity, human subject protection, procedures and method of analysis. Chapter 6 describes the analysis of the data and displays the outcomes. Chapter 7 will examine the findings and implications. Chapter 7 constitutes the bulk of this work and comprises an extended discussion of the notion of the entitlement model and its applicability to criminal behavior in general. However, it should be noted that this study's primary focus is to investigate personality constructs to determine their association with sexually violent behavior.

While the constructs of Machiavellianism and narcissism have been well researched, their relationship to sexual aggression among males has been somewhat neglected. It is anticipated that this work will contribute to the body of knowledge about sexual violence, and will advance the understanding of male sexual aggressors. The secondary purpose of this work is to relate the findings to concrete policy applications that might educate potential aggressors or victims, so that future sexual violence might be averted. The final goal of this work is to introduce the construct of entitlement, and to test its viability as a model for sexually aggressive behavior.

CHAPTER 2

Cognitive Structures and Entitled Belief Systems

COGNITIONS AND SCHEMAS

Cognitive science represents an amalgam of human thought and its attendant processes. Cognitive psychology represents the study of people's mental machinations. It includes perception, learning, memory, language efficiency, problem solving, decision-making, and reasoning (Kellogg, 1995). In processing perceptions, humans construct fluid, active mental models of the external, physical world. Kellogg (1995) described schemas as cognitive mechanisms that furnish people "with expectations about our environment and continually undergo modification through maturation and learning. Schemas direct the construction of all conscious experience in perceiving, remembering, imagining, and thinking" (p. 20).

Before reviewing the literature of sexual aggression, it is first necessary to briefly outline the framework of cognitive psychology, insofar as it pertains to the current study. In addition, two tenets of this work should be pointed out here:

> 1.) People tend to construct worldviews, or schemas, that can affect behavior.

> 2.) Machiavellianism and narcissism, and ultimately entitlement are learned and incorporated into schemas. Furthermore, the current study will examine the notion that entitlement is a cognitive structure that justifies, rationalizes or promotes sexually aggressive behavior.

It is necessary at this point to define some key terminology. *Cognitive schema* refers to how an individual perceives, categorizes and maps external perceptions. It also connotes an assignment of value to external events. Cognitive schema refers to "the organization of knowledge about a particular concept. The schema contains the features or attributes that are associated with a category membership" (Scholl, 1999, p. 2). A *script* is a particular kind of schema that exemplifies and determines how one behaves in a specific routine pastime (Abelson, 1981; Mandler, 1984; Kellogg, 1995). For example, a sexually aggressive male might hold a script as to how a first date should proceed: pick the woman up, take her to dinner, get her drunk, and have sexual intercourse with her in the back of his van.

Kellogg (1995) further noted that cognitive schemas are active and constructional in nature, bearing little resemblance to the stimulus-response passivity implied in strict behavioral notions of learning. Humans actively construct schemas, and the nature of schematic construction is determined by how people perceive the world. Furthermore, the event-driven scripting process indicates that cognitive styles bear on individual behavior.

Categories of Schemas

Scholl (1999) identified the following categories of schemas:

1.   Person schema: An individual constructs a framework about the attributes of a particular individual. One often attributes a personality to another person.
2.   Event schema: This is actually another term for the cognitive script. The event schema describes the processes by which we generally approach problems or tasks. People behave according to the programs of their schemas when confronting a particular stimulus.
3.   Role schema: In this schema, individuals possess certain expectations about how an individual occupying a certain role should behave. Humans tend to use this schema in different ways: Evaluation, Role-playing, Identification, and Prediction.

a. Evaluation: People tend to judge others who occupy a certain role (e.g. lawyer, professor, or sorority member). People compare these particular others to their culturally based role schema.

b. Role-playing: Individuals who assume a certain role (police officer, professor) often draw from the socially derived cognitive script as to how they should behave.

c. Identification: Humans tend to categorize others by their assumed role. People employ role schema to fit others into certain cognitive slots by comparing their observed behavior with the perceiver's role schema.

d. Prediction: Once the person categorizes another, he or she tends to assume that the object of perception will behave in a certain way that matches role schema (Scholl, 1999; Kellogg, 1995).

Finally, there is the self-schema, perhaps the most salient schema for this study. Self-schemas are based on generalizations about the self, and may be regarded as one's self-concept. The self-schema organizes knowledge about specific perceptions and serves as a mechanism that guides processing of new data and the retrieval of previously encoded stored knowledge. More simply, the self-schema is a generalized perception about the self, derived from experience. People construct self-schemas according to self-perceptions of their physical attributes, their traits and behavior (Sims & Lorenzi, 1992). Markus (1977) defined self-schemas as "cognitive generalizations about the self, derived from past experience, that organize and guide the processing of self-related information contained in the individual's experiences" (1977, p. 64). A self-schema is not only one's self-concept, but also determines how that self-concept is formed and maintained. A cognitive schema is a working mechanism, not just a mirror.

In this work, cognitive schema will be alternately termed as *scheme, style* or *cognitive construction*. All of these terms will encompass the full meaning of schema as a cognitive filter, map and organizational process that may ultimately affect behavior.

Schemas are developed through individual experiences. They evolve from simple mapping strategies into complex networks. They are on-going processes, influenced by both direct and indirect events

(Scholl, 1999). Consequently, cognitive schemas are heavily dependent upon social learning influences.

Schemas serve to categorize, organize and process incoming perceptions and enable quick decision-making. They are reinforced over time and through experiences, and are subject to sub-typing, or "re-fencing" (Allport, 1958). Re-fencing refers to a cognitive device whereby the individual perceives external evidence that is contrary to the existing schema. When a new, dissonant perception enters the mental field, the individual permits and acknowledges the new fact (allowing it through the metaphorical fence). The person then quickly closes the fence. To prohibit more jarringly dissonant information from entering the schema, the individual accepts a certain amount of exceptions to his or her world-view, but does not allow it to remain "dangerously open" (Allport, 1958, p. 23). Cognitive dissonance is further explored below.

The main point here is that schemas are elastic, within limited parameters. Equally important, this elasticity is purely utilitarian. An individual confronted with indisputable external stimuli that directly contradict his or her personal world-view has little choice but to acknowledge and make room for the dissonant new information. However, this acknowledgement is restricted by the overall boundaries of the schema. One will make exceptions for dissonant perceptions, but only within the overall rigid fence described by Allport. People make allowances for individual exceptions to their perception of the world, but they do not greatly alter their overall schemas. Naturally, schemas will differ in flexibility/rigidity between individuals.

The categorization function of the schema set forth by Allport has been explored in more recent literature. The tendencies to quickly categorize people and events (known as *heuristics*) were influenced by personality variables (Moore, Smith & Gonzalez, 1997). These authors reported that one's individual personality dimensions affect how one's heuristics are employed. Moreover, the nature of the person's judgment tends to be influenced by contextual cues. Differences among individuals can influence how a person employs the function of heuristic judgment when contextual cues trigger the schema's aspects that are salient to that particular variable. In other words, personality dimensions interact with schematic functioning.

The nature of schemas has also been investigated as they function in organizational behavior (Poole & Gray, 1990), leadership (Haines,

Hogg & Duck, 1997), body image (Altabe & Thompson, 1996), and as a model for understanding and treating personality disorders (Young & Lindeman, 1992).

Schemas, Rationalizations and Self-Serving Biases

One aspect of schemas that relates to this work is that of how people rationalize and justify observations about the world and the self. These compensatory processes are key to understanding how Machiavellianism and narcissism relate to the theoretical perspective of the schema. Allport (1937) detailed how humans engage in compensatory cognitions. According to Allport, people use self-justification and rationalization as "forms of compensation unconsciously designed not only to fool others but likewise to fool oneself" (p. 178). Self-justification is employed to allow the "beloved Ego" (p. 178), or self-concept, to win. While the triumph might not be legitimate in reality, the self will attempt to make it so in retrospect.

People compensate in a number of ways, according to Allport (1937). One might find extenuating circumstances to excuse the perceived failure. If necessary, these extenuations can become permanent, protective devices. For example, a man who perceives himself as a physical failure, perhaps small, weak and flabby, might rationalize that he is more artistic and sensitive than his more athletic peers. Allport distinguishes between the "sour grapes" and the "sweet lemons" justifications (p. 179). In the former, the individual disparages which he cannot attain. In the latter, he makes virtues out of flaws.

Another compensatory method is that of the immediate alibi. This is a short-term measure that can temporarily assuage the dissonance. As Allport (1937) wrote, "suspicion of incompetence is lulled; tension is removed....(but) sooner or later some more thoroughgoing type of compensation may have to be instituted" (p. 179). These are most likely situational in nature. A student who performs poorly on a single exam might blame an unfair professor's poorly worded test questions, or even her own lack of studying for that particular unit of material. Either option is more comfortable than the dissonance of acknowledging flaws in her basic intelligence or competence.

Furthermore, Allport (1937) explored the concept of "autistic thinking," or "fantasy" (pp. 179-180). Autism is defined by Allport as a compensatory mechanism that occurs when "an individual disregards completely the demands of his physical and social environment, withdrawing into himself to day-dream of success." (It should be noted that Allport's idea of *autism* is markedly different than the affliction detailed in the American Psychiatric Association's *Diagnostic and Statistical Manual IV* [1994]). In this fantasy-driven compensation, the individual might play various roles that allow him or her to escape a painful reality. Fantasy has been explored as an important cognitive element in the melange of motives driving the sexual aggressor (Ressler & Burgess, 1988).

It is contended here that these processes of rationalization all may be incorporated into one's schemas. Allport wrote that the "mature personality" is free of egocentricity. He contrasted the maturely developed person with the self-absorbed one:

> ...the garrulous Bohemian, egotistical, self-pitying, and prating of self-expression....Paradoxically, 'self-expression' requires the capacity to lose oneself in the pursuit of objectives, *not* (emphasis original) primarily referred to the self. Unless directed outward toward socialized and culturally compatible ends, unless absorbed in causes and goals that outshine self-seeking and vanity, any life seems dwarfed and immature" (1937, p. 213).

More recently, Greenwald (1980) identified several cognitive biases that individuals tend to use in formulating their self-concept, including overestimation of their own importance, the acceptance of praise for positive outcomes but denial of responsibility for negative ones, and the tendency to seek information that confirms their theories about themselves and adjust their autobiographical memories to coincide with their current self-concept. Cantor and Kihlstrom (1990) reviewed an array of cognitive biases that are based on the individual's need to maintain a positive self-representation, rather than on any objective reality. Wood (1989) maintained that people are self-serving and biased in their comparisons of themselves to others.

Allport (1937) considered self-directed belief structures as immature and maladaptive. They are also the primary focus of this work in its investigation of Machiavellian and narcissistic attitudes. This study will examine whether these self-directed beliefs, as manifested in the dimensions of Machiavellianism and narcissism might be a factor in (some) sexually aggressive behaviors.

Given the discussion of cognitions and schemas to this point, consider how the attitudinal belief structure of a sexual aggressor might evolve. To protect the self-schema from acknowledging dangerous information about the self, the individual will rationalize his (recall that this study is investigating male aggressors only) own behavior so it does not jar his existing schemas. The individual might engage in self-justification and rationalizations to compensate for personal flaws and failures.

It is contended that these elements of cognitive psychology directly apply to the social learning model of sexual aggression identified by Ellis (1989). One of the tenets that Ellis identified as integral to the social learning model was that rapists would generally hold more favorable attitudes toward sexual aggression, and overall violence, than would other men. This book examines the basis of this proposal—
that men learn to perceive and define situations in ways that either reinforce or repudiate sexually aggressive behavior. It is hypothesized that narcissism and Machiavellianism may measure these attitudinal definitions. Furthermore, it is asserted that these belief structures establish the foundation for the introduction of a new theoretical personality dimension. That dimension is *entitlement*.

One might wonder how all of this relates to sexual aggression. Simply, this: If individuals construct schemas that result in this behavior, there should be psychological characteristics that reflect this relationship. Furthermore, one might identify measurable attitudes linked to sexual aggression.

The links between attitudinal and belief configurations and sexual aggression have been examined in past research. For example, Malamuth, Heavey and Linz (1993) investigated the convergence of several attitudes and their role in sexually aggressive behavior. Malamuth et al. examined predictors such as Dominance Motive, Hostility Toward Women, Acceptance of Interpersonal Violence, and Antisocial Personality characteristics. In doing so, they suggested a prototypical model. That is, there exist critical variables that combine and interact to produce sexually aggressive behavior (Malamuth et al., 1993).

Similarly, other authors have demonstrated correlation between hostility and masculinity measures and sexually aggressive behavior (Malamuth, Sockloskie, Koss & Tanaka, 1991). As a final example,

Rapaport and Burkhart (1984) found significant predictors of sexual aggression among belief measures of Responsibility, Socialization, Acceptance of Interpersonal Violence, and other attitudinal scales.

The sexual aggression literature is rich with like examples. These will be further explored in the following chapter. It is sufficient here to introduce the multi-factored model of the sexual aggressor as a premise of this work.

SOCIAL COGNITIONS AND SOCIAL CONSTRUCTIONS

Brewer (1988) wrote, "...social cognition is the study of the interaction between internal knowledge structures—our mental representations of social objects and events—and new information about a specific person or social occasion" (p. 1). Brewer advanced a dual-processing model of cognitive impression structuring. Brewer criticized theories of impression formation that relied solely on the notion that humans tend to categorize other people, one at a time, and insert them into a convenient "mental slot" (p. 2). Instead, Brewer argued that social cognition should be conceived as organized around social categories, including "mental   representations of social attributes and classes of social events and social roles" (p. 3). Brewer distinguished between automatic processing of person-based impression formation and deeper cognitive processes that take into account existing schemas.

The essence of Brewer's model is that individuals do not always perceive new social objects (or people) as automatically categorized stimuli. Most times, the perceiver will rely on his or her own processing objectives. However the person perceives new stimuli, the method of categorization will be based on how the new knowledge will be incorporated into existing cognitive frameworks. Brewer also suggests that in general, people categorize because of information overload. That is, there are so many raw, perceived phenomena out there that humans must erect cognitive schemas to process them effectively (Brewer, 1988).

Medin (1988) offered a provocative alternative. He proposed that social categorization is undertaken because of too little, rather than too much information. While Medin laid out an impressive array of responses to the Brewer model, one of the most noteworthy for the purposes of this work was that

> Taking advantage of information in particular
> contexts also can improve predictions. For example, a
> mushroom found in the wild can be expected to have
> a much higher probability of being poisonous than
> one found in a grocery store. Similarly, people may
> behave differently at work that they do at home or at
> a party (p. 122).

This insight provides a perspective from which to view criminal behavior in general, and sexual aggression in particular. If the deviant conduct is based on the immediate social context, then one of the cognitive mechanisms governing behavior would necessarily be directly linked to immediate circumstances. Machiavellianism, as argued later, is such a mechanism.

Beall (1993) described social construction as a cognitive mechanism that is "concerned with how people come to understand the world around them and with how they come to define 'reality'" (p. 127). People tend to actively design, frame and erect their perceptions through the guiding prism of culture (Beall, 1993).

Social Cognitions and Narratives

Another perspective set forth by Gergen (1994) that bears on this study involves his model of the self-narrative. As Gergen described the self-narrative, the individual structures his or her self-concept as a "*discourse* (emphasis original) about the self" (1994, p. 185). Here Gergen distinguished between the development of personal cognitive structures and the self-narrative. Gergen made the distinction between individual cognitive schema and "conceptual categories" (p. 185) associated with self-narration. Gergen formulated the self-narrative as an encapsulation of "self-concepts, schemas, and self-esteem...with the self as a narration rendered intelligible within ongoing relationships" (p. 185).

In an earlier work, Gergen and Gergen (1988) offered a story-based concept of the social narrative, and of how humans cognitively order and process life events. These authors assert that people tend to categorize life experiences into traditional narrative, or story-telling templates. Gergen and Gergen related that humans filter raw life experiences into a framework that matches the universal conception of a good story. Specifically, people select important events, order them, establish causal links, develop plots, and hone them toward an end goal. They create suspense and drama, and generate narrative forms that may introduce danger (Gergen & Gergen, 1988).

Kellogg (1995) also noted the importance of narratives and stories in our culture. Bruner (1990) asserted the importance of understanding how cultural meaning is created and established by individuals through shared participation in archetypal, storied accounts of human existence.

This cognitive perspective is on point with earlier feminist perspectives that consider popular culture as a criminogenic agent that spawns and condones sexual aggression among males. Brownmiller (1975) detailed the myth of the heroic rapist.

> Throughout history no theme grips the masculine imagination with greater constancy and less honor than the myth of the heroic rapist. As man conquers the world, so too he conquers the female. Down through the ages, imperial conquest, exploits of valor and expressions of love have gone hand in hand with violence to women in thought and in deed (p. 289).

It may be argued that self-narration is a specific form of cognitive construction, rather than an altogether different mode of self-perception. In general, cognitive styles may be thought of as occurring at two levels: private and public. Kelly (1963) and Piaget (1948), to name two early theorists, detail private structuring. Kelly's (1963) work also ties in with public cognitions and Gergen's (1994) components of the self-narrative schema. Both modes are pertinent to the current study, and both will be discussed here.

Private Constructions

As Piaget (1948) conceived the cognitive framework, humans engage in adjustive behaviors while interacting with the environment, which he termed "assimilation" and "accommodation" (as cited in Van Zander, 1984, p. 117). Assimilation refers to the process of receiving raw external phenomena and coding it so it fits to the existing cognitive scheme. While Piaget was referring to the cognitive development of the child, Kelly (1963) suggested that adults also engage in assimilation. In addition, Allport's (1958) ideas of human learning, attitudes and beliefs, and prejudice assume a cognitive style of assimilation that transcends childhood.

Assimilation can at times lead to "stretching" (Vander Zanden, 1984, p. 117) a scheme to fit the new perceptions. When the child is confronted with new information that does not conform to the perceived vision of the world, according to Piaget, he or she must reorganize the model to better fit the world. In this way, the child's cognitive map is continually reshaped into (supposedly) an increasingly efficacious system.

"Accommodation," according to Piaget (1948) refers to modifying an existing cognitive scheme to better fit reality. Vander Zanden wrote, "in accommodation, preceding structures become a part of later structures...consequently, each stage in cognitive development witnesses the emergence of new organizational components. And each stage is in turn the starting point of the next stage" (Vander Zanden, 1984, p. 117). Therefore, the key difference between assimilation and accommodation lies within the degree to which existing cognitive schemas are modified to incorporate perceived realities.

While Piaget (1948) made these assertions about the developing child, Kelly (1963) made a similar contention about humans in general. However, Kelly also made the point that a reorganization of an existing superordinate construct (which may be argued to be equivalent to Piaget's accommodation of the scheme) is an uncomfortable, aversive task. He maintained that the individual becomes dependent upon and invested into his or her cognitive system, and that overhauling it could be damaging to the existing structure. Kelly (1963) submitted that one might opt to forego major alterations on his or her system, and risk the maintenance of an imprecise but familiar and comfortable worldview. This idea of a self-construct system serves as an effective way to conceptualize the existence and functions of schemas and belief dimensions.

Public Constructions and Personal Narratives

Kelly (1963) considered public constructions as a certain type of system that is widely shared and accessible to the members of a culture. He contended that certain scientific bodies of knowledge attained the status of "realm" (1963, p. 9). That is, knowledge fields such as natural science and psychology exist as public realms. They are communicable and universal constructions. These scientific disciplines form a generalized body of knowledge that is shared by members of the disciplines.

Furthermore, as the generalized bodies of knowledge increase, it becomes apparent that the distinctions between them are artificial and contrived. Boundaries between the realms blur, and they might overlap. The elements of the realms become generalized knowledge, and at that point the constructions are public. In his example of physiology and psychology realms, Kelly (1963) wrote, "Are those 'psychological facts' or are they 'physiological facts'? *Where do they really belong?* (emphasis added)....The answer is, of course that the events upon which facts are based hold no institutional loyalties. They are in the public domain" (p. 10).

Kelly's notion of public constructions may be likened to Gergen's (1994) concept of the cultural narrative. Like Kelly, Gergen asserted that generalized fields of knowledge permeate the atmosphere of a particular culture. Kelly's model proposed the viability of shared knowledge integrating itself into a common realm. Gergen advanced this conceptualization to include shared cultural stories and themes. Gergen wrote, "this is a story about stories—and most particularly, stories of the self" (1994, p. 185). As an individual lives life and gains experiences, he or she absorbs various types of stories. Whether they are derived from folklore, mythology, family, or popular culture, these organized accounts of human existence bombard and permeate the individual's schematic exterior shield, which perceives and then categorizes them into the self-concept.

Stories, according to Gergen (1994), are culturally ubiquitous. Humans read books, watch television and movies, listen to music, and generally absorb numerous cultural accounts of human existence through their everyday perceptions. Gergen speculated, reasonably enough, that this ongoing conditioning affects how people define and organize the intimate relationships that form their own lives. Stated another way, the human tendency to construct personal schemas is assisted by the packaged characteristics of stories. This work asserts that storied narratives (pre-constructed by society) save people the labor of categorizing, judging and processing the many new perceptions they encounter every day. It is feasible that culturally-based, storied narratives may be assimilated into one's mental rules and frameworks with less friction than raw phenomena.

Kelly (1963) suggested that one of the reasons people employ schemas is to incorporate perceived phenomena into their established superordinate constructs. Moreover, communicability of others' personal constructs leads to Kelly's notion of "public constructs" (p. 9).

Kelly wrote, "our public construction systems for understanding other people's personal constructs are becoming more precise and more comprehensive" (p. 9). Relating this to Gergen's (1994) notions, one may consider the storied narrative as a public construct, widely shared, and disseminated by a story-laden culture.

Thus far, this work has reviewed the general nature of cognitive schemas and the role that social constructions play in their formation. Attention now turns to other cognitive elements, specifically, dissonance, social comparisons and social learning. These elements will be incorporated into the review of the sexual aggression literature. Furthermore, it will be argued that these cognitive components play a role in the formations of the belief structures of Machiavellianism and narcissism. Later, this work will examine the relationships of Machiavellianism and narcissism with sexual aggression. An understanding of the basic cognitive elements is also necessary to understand the conceptual foundation of entitlement, which will conclude the literature and theoretical review for this study.

COGNITIVE DISSONANCE AND SOCIAL COMPARISONS

Cognitive Dissonance

As individuals live their lives, they encounter events that do not fit in with their schemas. The most easily recognizable example is when the observer perceives some kind of person or object that does not fit his or her stereotype, and thus feels threatened, or at least uneasy, until the discordant observation is somehow resolved. Festinger (1957) termed this aversion to assimilating frictional phenomena into a schema "cognitive dissonance." As Festinger wrote, "the individual strives toward consistency within himself...his opinions and attitudes...tend to exist in clusters that are internally consistent" (p. 1). Festinger further proposed that dissonance motivates the individual to reduce this uncomfortable cognitive state, and attempt to achieve one of equilibrium, or consonance. Festinger also hypothesized that an individual in a dissonant state will avoid circumstances and situations that may aggravate this uncomfortable condition (1957). Allport (1937) noted this and theorized about some of the compensatory devices discussed above, such as re-fencing. Bem (1970) similarly pointed out that people might hold onto existing belief structures even in the face of repeated falsifications. The observer recognizes exceptions but subtypes them as rarities and maintains a central category of "all the rest of them" (p. 9).

Festinger (1957) was among the first to recognize the importance of "cognitive elements" (p. 19) in self-constructs. Aside from the self-perceptual element (that is inherent in his discussion of maintaining cognitive equilibrium, or consonance), Festinger added the elements of environment and behavior (1957). One attempts to avoid or reduce dissonance because it is, by definition, psychologically uncomfortable. For example, a man may consider himself as fair-minded about equal rights for women; he may have a vague belief that women should have equal opportunity in the workplace. But he may dislike it when he gets a new female supervisor. While the man may attempt to rationalize this inconsistency ("it is because she is under-qualified, not because she is a woman"), he may fail to do so for one reason or another. Therefore the cognitive irritant will continue its existence and eventually produce psychological discomfort. The male employee in this example may avoid contact with his female boss and refuse to discuss her with his compatriots.

Importantly then, Festinger (1957) linked actual behavior to the maintenance of consonance. As he wrote, "cognitive dissonance can be seen as an antecedent condition which leads to activity oriented toward dissonance reduction just as hunger leads to activity oriented toward hunger reduction" (1957, p. 3). Moreover, Aronson (1968) proposed that dissonance stems primarily from the role of the self— "If dissonance exists, then it is the result of cognitions inconsistent with the self-concept" (p. 23, cited in Elliot & Devine, 1994).

Furthermore, Devine,   Monteith,   Zuwerink, and Eliot (1991) reported that the magnitude of psychological discomfort experienced by the individual was greater and more specific when that person violated deeply held beliefs and guidelines. The more self-relevant and self-defining these violated internal standards were, the greater the dissonance, both in depth and in specificity. Therefore, if dissonance motivates behavior, as Festinger proposed and Eliot and Devine (1994) demonstrated, it follows that belief structures held about the self will influence how that behavior manifests itself. Elliot and Devine (1994) wrote, "people who are emotionally invested in grandiose self-views are the most aggressive, particularly in response to an esteem threat" (p. 227). These investigators concluded that additional research was needed to investigate whether various levels of self-relevance translated into different reduction strategies.

This point is important because self-relevance is such a salient component of the narcissist and the Machiavellian, as will be discussed below. Both dimensions are grounded in the maintenance of self-interest and self-image. Self-absorption seems to be a deeply internalized standard for both of these belief structures. Research into how self-absorption can lead to sexual aggression is warranted to supplement understanding into how cognitive structuring is related to antisocial behavior.

The aggressor's schemas function in a manner that is excessively self-serving. Machiavellianism and narcissism are two manifestations of this. This study seeks to find out if sexual aggression is one behavioral result.

Social Comparisons

Some of the sexual aggression literature reviewed below embodies the ideas of dissonance and social comparisons. Furthermore, the introduction of the entitlement construct below is based partly on the dynamics of social comparisons. Therefore, it might be helpful at this point to introduce the idea of social comparison and examine how dissonance plays a role in its functioning.

Festinger's work on social comparisons is pertinent here as an example of how social cognition relates to behavior. Cognitive styles can and do drive behavior. As an example, Festinger offered data from Lipset, Lazarsfeld, Barton & Linz (1954, as cited in Festinger, 1957) and Blau (1953, as cited in Festinger, 1957) that demonstrated the tendency of individuals to obtain consensus with others in order to reduce dissonance. That is, people sought agreement with others, through social comparisons, in order to ameliorate cognitive discomfort. Festinger maintained that a person burdened with dissonance will attempt to find others who agree with the cognitive phenomena he or she is trying to attain. Failing that, the dissonant will attempt to sway others to his or her opinion (social communication is a central component of the process of attempted dissonance reduction).

Wood (1989) summarized Festinger's (1954) tenets of the social comparison process. People have a proclivity to assess their own abilities and opinions. In the absence of objective, physical standards, they will engage in social comparison. That is, they will evaluate themselves against others, preferably others that are similar to them. Also, individuals will endeavor to be as accurate as possible in constructing their worldview. Furthermore, humans feel pressured to continue to improve their abilities (and cognitive styles) in a "unidirectional drive upward" (Festinger, 1954, as cited in Wood, 1989, p. 231).

Wood (1989) also pointed out the importance of the social context in which the comparisons occur. Wood (1989) described surrounding dimensions as peripheral social aspects that are involved in social comparisons, but are not the main focus of them. For example, a male college student may be conducting a self-evaluation on his attractiveness to women. He may not only compare himself to his friends and their dating activities, but also on whether his peers are wealthy, or perhaps whether they have greater opportunities to meet women because they do not study as much as the self-evaluator. The student reaches to tangential circumstances in comparison to protect the self-concept. That is, to avoid dissonance, this student really had to reach beyond the immediate object of perception (in this case, a popular peer) and bring in compensatory items (wealth, better opportunities). Obviously, this form of social comparison incorporates a strong rationalization component.

Wood (1989) challenged Festinger's (1957) notion that humans strive to attain the most accurate worldview through social comparison. She argued that people tend to harbor motives that are linked to self-evaluation and self-enhancement. These motives will impact on how self-comparisons are conducted. Wood wrote, "...there is growing evidence that people are not unbiased; they often harbor unrealistically positive views of themselves and bias information in a self-serving manner" (p. 232).

If Machiavellianism and narcissism are representative dimensions of self-directed beliefs, it is expected that they will play a key role in the social comparison process. Self-serving ideations of the self are integral components of Machiavellianism and narcissism. Whether their role in social comparisons is functional or dysfunctional, or whether they relate to sexually aggressive behavior might provide insight into whether self-serving behavior is a worthy topic for future research.

Like everyone else, the aggressor has a schema about the roles of himself and of others. Much of the preceding discussion has dealt (albeit superficially) with how cognitions might be formed and how they tend to function. The crucial premise of this work is that the cognitive schemas of the narcissist and the Machiavellian are essentially self-serving. One result of this self-serving dimension of the schema is sexual aggression.

THE BIG FIVE PERSONALITY MODEL

The factor model of personality known as the Big Five was developed over a period of decades by various scholars (Cattell, 1933; Fiske, 1949; Tupes & Christal, 1961; Tupes & Kaplan, 1961; Norman, 1963; Borgatta, 1964; Costa & McCrae, 1985; Digman & Takemoto-Chock, 1981a; Goldberg, 1981; John, Angleitner, & Ostendorf, 1988; McCrae & Costa, 1989, as cited by Digman, 1997). In its simplest form, this model consists of five traits of human personality that are perhaps more descriptive than developmental. That is, the Big Five model might represent an efficient organization of stable, universal personality dimensions but does not offer insights into the development of personality, nor does it account for individual behavioral exceptions to these traits (McAdams, 1992). However, the model remains a useful and popular conceptual framework for personality investigators (Digman, 1997; Digman & Inouye, 1986; Sadowski & Cogburn, 1997).

Elements of the Big Five Personality Model

While there is some disagreement over the exact meaning of each factor, there is general agreement that the Big Five model comprises the following traits (Digman, 1986).

> 1.) Extraversion or Surgency: talkative or silent; sociable or reclusive; adventurous or cautious.
> 2.) Agreeableness: good-natured or irritable; mild/gentle or headstrong; cooperative or negative; not jealous or jealous.
> 3.) Conscientiousness: responsible or undependable; persevering or quitting/fickle; fussy/tidy-careless;

scrupulous-unscrupulous. Also described as goal-orientation and ambition or lazy and negligent (www.fmarion.edu/~pesonality/corr/big5/traits.html).
3.) Neuroticism/Emotional Stability: calm or anxious; composed or excitable; non-hypochondriacal or hypochondriacal; poised or nervous/tense.
4.) Openness to Experience or Intellect/Culture: imaginative or simple/direct; artistically sensitive or not; intellectual or non-reflective and narrow-minded; polished and refined or boorish (p. 117).

The Big Five, Narcissism and Machiavellianism

If the Big Five taxonomy encompasses the most reliable and consistent factors of personality, it should follow that the cognitive styles of narcissism and Machiavellianism should be embedded in the model. These constructs are more closely examined below in Chapter 4, but their essential components merit limited discussion here in order to demonstrate their relationship to the Big Five model.

Machiavellianism is a personality dimension that is characterized by the use of deceit, guile, manipulativeness, and distrust of others. The Machiavellian seeks to gain advantage over others in any interpersonal exchange. This self-interested individual perceives others as potentially hostile agents who threaten the Machiavellian's need to constantly seek a tactical edge over other people. The Mach ignores ideas of conventional morality and regards other people as objects to be used in an ongoing mission to come out on top in all of the challenges offered by an unfriendly world (Christie & Geis, 1970).

The narcissist, as conceptualized in the current study, is a self-aggrandizing individual who lacks empathy for others. This person believes that he or she is special and deserving of excessive and unearned admiration and maintains an exaggerated self-concept. The narcissist is exploitative and consistently demonstrates haughty and arrogant attitudes (American Psychological Association, *Diagnostic and Statistical Manual IV*, 4th Edition). Furthermore, this construct is characterized by a continued quest for validation of the inflated self-perception.

If one considers the Big Five as the elements of personality, and Machiavellianism and narcissism as particular formations of these elements, it is feasible to trace these constructs back to one or more of the original components. Machiavellianism may best be conceptualized as a manifestation of low Conscientiousness, in the scrupulous/unscrupulous sense of the trait. (Interestingly, the Mach might well score higher in Conscientiousness in the goal-orientation meaning). The Mach is most likely an unreliable and irresponsible person, as he or she is driven primarily by self-interest.

The Machiavellian tendency to distrust others also suggests a tendency to possess a low magnitude of Agreeableness. The Mach's cynicism reflects a lack of trust and therefore a low likelihood of cooperation with others, unless the Mach cooperates for underlying, selfish reasons, or if he or she perceives the cooperative partners as competent accomplices in a deviant activity, such as cheating (Bogart, Geis, Levy & Zimbardo, 1970).

The narcissist's belief structure appears to draw from the Extraversion/Surgency trait to the extent that this individual is exhibitionistic and sociable in his or her quest for admiration. The narcissist's twist on Extraversion/Surgency is most likely represented by a strutting grandiosity that is aimed at supplementing an exaggerated self-concept. While narcissism might seem to be positively associated with Extraversion/Surgency in this sense, it should be noted that narcissism probably represents a façade of healthy sociability and does not represent a true affection for others. The narcissist is extraverted and surgent to the degree to which this component satisfies a dysfunctional self-aggrandizement.

Narcissism, like Machiavellianism, reflects a low degree of Conscientiousness, in the social responsibility conceptualization of the component. The narcissist tends to lack empathy for others and primarily considers others as objects whose main purpose is to admire and aggrandize him or her. The narcissist's sense of entitlement to favorable treatment and compliance indicates a low sense of social conformity or responsibility. This individual is primarily concerned with on-going validation of an exaggerated sense of self-importance, and this tendency runs counter to the scrupulous and orderliness associated with Conscientiousness.

The Big Five model represents a consistent taxonomy of traits that have emerged through factor analysis studies (www.carleton.ca/~tpychyl/01138/BigFive.html) and can be considered a reliable, descriptive blueprint of personality. It is argued here that cognitive styles such as narcissism and Machiavellianism might be constructed from elements of the Big Five model. Moreover, it is possible that investigating how these traits interact and combine could provide a new venue for research into criminal behavior. The current study does not even touch on Neuroticism/Emotional Stability or Openness/Intellect/Culture. Future investigation into the Big Five model might prove to be fruitful for criminologists researching human deviance.

CHAPTER 3

Sexual Aggression: An Overview

As stated in Chapter 1, this work defines sexual aggression as a wide-ranging concept that includes milder behaviors such as forcing a kiss on another up to and including forcible, violent rape. The conceptualization also includes the use of alcohol or drugs to coerce another into sexual acts. This definition is consistent with much of the sexual aggression literature and is appropriate to the Koss sexual aggression scale (1982).

This section reviews sexual aggression literature as it pertains to social or external variables associated with coercion and later with personal, internal components. The former includes membership in athletics or fraternal organizations; the latter includes attitudinal and personality measures. It will be shown that strictly environmental correlates do not clearly account for sexually aggressive behavior. An approach that incorporates multidimensional personal attributes and social variables might be the most appropriate venue of research.

STUDIES IN SEXUAL AGGRESSION

Fraternities, Athletics and Other Social Variables

Boeringer (1996) investigated the influences of fraternity membership, participation in collegiate athletics, and sex composition housing arrangements on sexual aggression among male undergraduates.

Employing a sample of 477 male undergraduates, Boeringer (1996) administered scales measuring the dependent variable of sexual aggression using the Malamuth (1981) Likelihood to Rape or use Force (LR/LF scale) and a modification of the Koss (1982) Sexual Experiences Survey (SES). Besides measuring the tendency to use physical force in sexual encounters, these scales also addressed the use of drugs and/or alcohol, as well as verbal coercion to obtain sex. These authors also measured the effects of the correlates of fraternity membership, participation in athletics, and same-sex dormitories on reported sexual aggression (Boeringer, 1996).

Boeringer (1996) reported that fraternity members used intoxicants and nonphysical coercion significantly more than did non-fraternity members to pressure females into sexual relations. (Recall the earlier model of sexual aggression as a continuum that includes such behaviors that fall short of forcible rape [Koss & Oros, 1982; Scully, 1990]). Boeringer found no significant difference between the two groups for the use of physical coercion. Boeringer also found that athletes scored higher on all of the dependent variables, and scored significantly higher on the likelihood to use force (self-report). Male athletes were more likely to report that they would use force to obtain sex if they were in a no-penalty situation, that is, if they were assured of getting away with it. Importantly, Boeringer reported that his data did not indicate that athletes were more likely to actually *commit* acts of sexual aggression. Boeringer suggested that the directionality of this association is unclear. It is possible that males who are more likely to report a willingness to use force to obtain sex may also happen to be more likely to engage in varsity sports, or that there exists within the social context of athletics a propensity toward sexually aggressive attitudes.

Schwartz and Nogrady (1996) conducted a study addressing similar variables. The researchers administered Gilmartin-Zena's Acceptance of Rape Myths (ARM) scale and Koss' Sexual Experiences

Survey (SES). In addition, the investigators asked a number of correlate items pertaining to other behaviors, such as alcohol/drug use and participation in campus organizations. Counter to their expectations, and in contrast to the Boeringer (1996) study, Schwartz and Nogrady (1996) reported no significant difference between fraternity and non-fraternity groups in rape myth acceptance. Further, fraternity membership was not an explanatory variable for sexually coercive behavior. However, the authors assert that this may suggest that social processes supporting the sexual victimization of women are not unique to fraternities, but that other groups on campus might foster the same belief systems. Schwartz and Nogrady also found alcohol consumption and perceived peer activity (regarding sexual coercion) to be positively correlated with self-reported tendency to sexually aggress.

Koss and Gaines (1993) also investigated the role of alcohol use, athletics and fraternity affiliation in the prediction of sexual aggression. In a study that used the Hostility Toward Women scale as another independent variable along with the aforementioned variables, the researchers reported that overall, sexual aggression was the result of multiple variables. The investigators employed a sample of 530 undergraduate males, including 140 athletes from various varsity sports. Koss and Gaines were unable to find significant support for the correlation between fraternity affiliation and sexual aggression if the variable of alcohol consumption was controlled.

Koss and Gaines (1993) reported multiple variables contributing to sexual aggression, the most significant ones being alcohol and nicotine use. The researchers reported that affiliation with revenue-generating sports (as opposed to being spectators or being involved with informal sports) was the third most significant predictor of sexual aggression out of 14 variables. However, the association was weak (r^2= .11).

A related study by Boeringer, Shehan, and Akers (1991) investigated the roles of social learning, acceptance of rape myths, and fraternity membership as independent variables to explain sexual aggression. The independent variables of social learning included items pertaining to perceived peer activities regarding sexually coercive behavior. These researchers found that fraternity members were more likely to employ nonphysical coercion and intoxicants against women as sexual strategies. However, they demonstrated no significant difference from non-fraternity members in the use of physical coercion.

These mixed findings suggest that the effects of social variables (i.e., alcohol intake, fraternal membership or athletic involvement) on sexually aggressive behavior are unclear. Furthermore, they tend to account more for nonphysical coercion than physical violence. It is apparent that individual, internal variables should be sought to better understand sexual coercion.

Attitudes, Cognitions and Personality Variables

Malamuth, Heavey and Linz (1993) developed and tested a "confluent" (p. 63) or interactive model of sexual aggression. These authors proposed that there exist certain dimensions, or "risk variables" (p. 63), that interact to contribute to sexual aggression. Malamuth and his colleagues contend that a multidimensional model holds the most promise to understanding sexually coercive behaviors of males against females. Drawing from a variety of personality/attitudinal dimensions (hostility toward women, acceptance of interpersonal violence, dominance), a physiological predictor (tumescent arousal to rape), and pathological characteristics (measuring sociopathy), these authors also incorporated the notion of domain specificity. That is, they asserted the need to differentiate between general aggression and aggressiveness against women in particular. Using a variety of analysis techniques, Malamuth et al. (1993) reported support for their confluence model. Of particular interest to the current study is their finding that "part of the connection between the hostile masculinity path and coercive behaviors toward women may be explained by a general factor that might be described as a reflection of narcissism, particularly the maladaptive components." (1993, p. 87). Malamuth and his colleagues also speculated whether the narcissistic component of low empathy might be clearly linked to their overall model of sexual aggression.

Malamuth, Sockloskie, Koss and Tanaka (1991) conducted a study using a national sample of subjects ($n = 2,972$). Malamuth and his colleagues tested a number of attitudinal and personal history variables to determine the personality characteristics of the aggressors (both sexual *and* non-sexual). The attitudinal variables included hostile masculinity, rape myth acceptance, coerciveness and social isolation. The personal history factors included parental violence, child abuse, and past delinquency. Using these as risk variables, Malamuth et al. reported significant support for their multi-factorial model of sexual aggression. In a later study that was not as large-scale, but was perhaps more on point with the current study, Dean and Malamuth (1997) measured dominance and self-centeredness among other attitudinal variables against dimensions of sexual aggression and found significant correlation.

Another study by Rando, Rogers and Powell (1998) investigated the role of cognitive dimensions or attitudes that support sexually aggressive behavior. These authors also addressed the idea of gender role conflict in sexual aggression. They reported that their results suggested that feelings of being demeaned or belittled by women or of inadequacy are specifically related to sexual aggression. The authors reported that gender role conflict among males was significantly associated with hostile masculinity.

Rapaport and Burkhart (1984) studied a sample of 201 undergraduate males to test the personality characteristics of sexually coercive men. Among the characteristics measured were socialization (So), responsibility (Re), and empathy (Em) as derived from the California Personality Inventory (CPI). Rapaport and Burkhart employed these variables to examine one or more dimensions of sociopathy. They reported that low socialization and responsibility scores were the most strongly correlated with self-reported sexual aggression. Low scores on these scales indicate a lack of social conscience, irresponsibility, and immaturity. Rapaport and Burkhart stated, "...sexually coercive males act on a system of values wherein females are perceived as adversaries....Sexual encounters become the setting for the behavioral expression of this combination of values and personality traits" (p. 220). The discussion of Machiavellianism below reveals a similar worldview for those who are highly Machiavellian (or "high Machs," as Christie and Geis [1970] term these individuals).

In a related study, Kosson and Kelly (1997) investigated the role of personality dimensions in the prediction of self-reported sexual aggression among college men. Using a sample of 378 males, these authors measured the impact of sociopathy (with the Psychopathy Checklist or PCL), socialization (So), and narcissism (the Narcissistic Personality Inventory or NPI). The authors found that narcissism and low socialization (So) both contributed to predicting sexual aggression, but along different dimensions. Narcissism tended to be associated with the use of argument to attain sexual gratification, as well as the abuse of status or authority. High-narcissism/low socialization scores were reported as strong predictors of sexual aggression, accounting for 62% of subjects reporting any form of sexual aggression.

Hersh and Gray-Little (1998) studied the relationships among dimensions of sociopathy, rape-supportive attitudes, and self-reported sexual aggression among college males. Among other scales used to measure rape-supportive attitudes, these authors employed the Schedule for Nonadaptive and Adaptive Personality (SNAP). SNAP is a multidimensional instrument that, in this case, was used to measure the sociopathic characteristics of Aggressiveness, Impulsivity and Manipulativeness. The last is significant to this study because manipulativeness is also a characteristic of Machiavellianism, discussed below. Hersh and Gray-Little (1998) also tested their 198 male college students for empathy. Low empathy is another component of Machiavellianism. These authors found that the subjects who had self-reported higher levels of sexual aggression also reported themselves to be less empathic and more manipulative.

Related investigations include: the links between masculinity dimensions and attitudes toward date rape (Truman & Tokar, 1996); perceptions of sexually aggressive vs. non-aggressive men's attitudes toward acquaintance rape (Yescavage, 1999); expectations of men and women regarding sexual aggression among fraternity and sorority members (Nurius & Norris, 1996); and, another multidimensional model similar to Malamuth and his colleagues that included measures of attraction to sexual aggression and of anger (Calhoun & Bernat, 1997). While a number of these studies also incorporated some of the social variables discussed above, they focused mainly on internal belief structures of the participants. Overall, the findings from these studies suggest that this approach is more productive in predicting sexual aggression than is a focus strictly on social variables, such as fraternal membership or athletic participation. (A notable exception to this is the significant effect of alcohol and nicotine use reported by Koss [1993]). However, because the literature on social variables remains unclear, the proposed study will address them as well.

Ellis (1985) proposed an alternative to the attitudinal or belief structure model. In this model, called the Synthesized Theory of Rape, Ellis (1985) offered four propositions about sexual violence. The first two are:

1.) Both the sex drive and a drive to possess and control motivate rape (1985, p. 57)

2.) Most of the behavior surrounding the commission of rape is learned experientially through operant conditioning, rather than as a result of modeling or changes in attitudes (1985, p. 65).

The third and fourth propositions are related to psychoevolutionary and physiological theories, and exceed the scope of the current study. The first proposition is of interest in that it points to inherent human drives as contributory agents to sexually aggressive behavior. Admittedly, this innate view of drives may seem contrary to the current study's premise about the relationship of learned schematic frameworks to sexual aggression. However, it is interesting that many of the attitudinal scales employed in the literature seem to tap into the concept of the "drive to possess and control." Whether one argues that drives are purely inherent or, conversely, that they might be at least partially acquired by learning, both perspectives acknowledge the relationship between the desire for control/possession and sexual aggression. The studies reviewed above employed scales that measured domination, hostility, masculinity, and acceptance of interpersonal violence. Most importantly, the element of manipulation is a central component of Machiavellianism, and relates directly to Ellis's (1985) proposition. While the current work asserts that the sexual aggressor's manipulative and controlling tendencies are more related to learning and cognition than the inborn drives offered by Ellis, it is perhaps significant that both perspectives recognized this aspect of behavior. Manipulation and control should thus be regarded as key components of any sexual aggression model.

In the second, more problematic proposition, Ellis (1985) considered the social learning notions of sexual aggression as secondary to operant learning. Ellis proposed that men rape because they are driven to do so (as set forth in proposition one) and will continue to rape (or engage in other types of sexual aggression) because they are intermittently reinforced to do so. Ellis (1985) did not necessarily discount the influence of modeling and attitudinal formation, but maintained that they are not as important as experiential learning.

The main problem with this proposition is that it does not explain why some men are not sexually aggressive. Ellis assumes that innate drives constitute the motivation to rape, and men who rape are reinforced in some manner to do so. This proposition appears flawed. If men are naturally selected to be sexually aggressive, why are not all men rapists? And why are rapes violent above and beyond the mere act of copulation? (e.g. Ressler and Burgess, 1988; see also Groth, 1979). Therefore, the current study diverges with Ellis's model at this point and subscribes to the attitudinal/cognitive style model of sexual aggression. It is premised that men learn to rape, not by operant conditioning, as suggested by Ellis, but by cognitive constructions that manifest themselves in general belief structures that support sexual violence. Furthermore, there is some empirical support that certain types of modeling, such as viewing violent pornography, can contribute to men's belief in rape myths (Malamuth & Check, 1985). Ellis, in contrast, disputes the idea of rape myths by suggesting that they might contain an element of truth.

From the literature reviewed in this section, several attitudinal themes have emerged as being associated with male sexual violence or coercion. They include low empathy, hostility towards women, manipulation and control, self-centeredness, low social conscience, poor socialization, and rape-supportive attitudes of the social or cultural milieu. Moreover, from the cognitive literature it may be argued that the social cognitions might result in maladaptive biases that are a function of excessive self-interest. Furthermore, it is contended that the social/cultural storied narrative construct proposed by Gergen and Gergen (1988; see also Gergen, 1994) meshes with Brownmiller's (1975) description of the "heroic rapist" and other rape myths that are supported by the aggressor.

The current study will further examine how cognitive styles (manifested in dimensional aspects of narcissism and Machiavellianism) affect behavior, specifically sexual aggression, and most specifically sexually coercive behavior. In contemplating Machiavellianism, narcissism, and the introduced entitlement concept in light of the sexual aggression literature, this work will link learned cognitive styles (as displayed through the constructs discussed in Chapter 2) with sexually aggressive behavior. In addition, demographic or social correlates (distinct from the scales) will be examined. These items are fraternity membership, athletic affiliation, age, number of credits earned, and self-reported sexual experience in relation to one's peers.

CHAPTER 4

Machs, Narcs, Sexual Aggressors and the Entitled

MACHIAVELLIANISM

In their introduction to the concept of Machiavellianism as a personality structure, Christie and Geis (1970) wrote, "since the publication of *The Prince* in 1532, the name of its author has come to designate the use of guile, deceit, and opportunism in interpersonal relations...the 'Machiavellian' is someone who views and manipulates others for his [*sic*] own purposes" (p. 1). Christie and Geis also operationalized Machiavellianism and developed a psychometric scale based upon the writings of Niccolo Machiavelli.

This section will first review Christie and Geis's conceptualization and operationalization of Machiavellianism. A review and discussion of related literature follows. In particular, their relationship with sexual aggression is discussed. Furthermore, this chapter introduces and reviews narcissism and also relates that dimension to sexual violence. Finally, the construct of entitlement will be introduced as a theoretical explanatory component of male sexual aggression. Entitlement depends on Machiavellianism and narcissism for its key aspects.

Christie and Geis (1970) observed that the psychopathological model significantly swayed treatises about the characteristics of those who exercise power over others. These authors asserted that a psychopathological approach towards understanding powerful manipulators was deficient. Indeed, these authors stated that adoption of a hypothetical role model was the best means to delve into the nature of a powerful, controlling individual. They asked themselves "what abstract characteristics must someone who is effective in controlling others have? What kind of person should he (*sic*) be?" (p. 3).

Christie and Geis set forth the following characteristics as crucial elements of such an individual:

> 1. "A relative lack of affect in interpersonal relationships" (p. 3). These authors wrote that the manipulator's ability to control others is aided by his or her perception of others as objects to be used, rather than as individual people worthy of empathy. It is difficult to implement psychological influence over others with whom one has developed an affective, empathic perception, or relationship.
>
> 2. "A lack of concern with conventional morality" (p. 3). These authors maintain that controlling, manipulative individuals embrace a utilitarian, rather than a moral worldview in their interpersonal interactions. Christie and Geis concede that conventional morality is a nebulous concept, but base their definition on what an average person would consider as common, but wrong behaviors, such as cheating, lying or other types of deceit.
>
> 3. "A lack of gross psychopathology" (pp. 3-4). Because the manipulative individual must make rational readings of others in order to transact his or her controlling strategies, these authors assert that "most neurotics and psychotics" (p. 3) would fail in this endeavor. Christie and Geis wrote,
>
> Note that we are not suggesting that manipulators are the epitome of mental health; we were proposing that their contact with at least the more objective aspects of reality would have to be, almost by definition, within the normal range (p. 4).

4. " Low ideological commitment" (p. 4). The manipulator is intent on achieving specific objectives or tasks, and is not concerned with overarching philosophical or ideological goals. Put another way, the manipulator may be thought of as operating in a tactical (short-term benefit), rather than a strategic (long-term goal achievement) manner.

Machiavellianism and the Anti-Social Personality Disorder

It is interesting to note that Christie and Geis's (1970) characteristics bear some resemblance to the Antisocial Personality Disorder as outlined in the American Psychiatric Association's *Diagnostic and Statistical Manual IV* (1994). Despite the third characteristic's caveat that the Machiavellian manipulator does not suffer from any obvious psychopathology, the similarities of the first two aspects are striking enough to mention here. The *DSM IV* classification criteria for sociopathy (a term used, for the purposes of this work, interchangeably with the Antisocial Personality Disorder) include "failure to conform with social norms with respect to lawful behavior" (p. 649), "deceitfulness" (p. 650), and "lack of remorse, as indicated by being indifferent to or rationalizing having hurt...another" (p. 650). Indeed, Skinner (1989) reported a moderate correlation between sociopathy and Machiavellianism in a study of 113 undergraduates who completed the Eysenck Personality Questionnaire and the Mach V scale. Also, Rapaport and Burkhart (1984) cite evidence that the Anti-Social Personality disorder is the primary clinical assessment of rapists (Armentrout & Hauer, 1978; Groth, 1979; Rada, 1979; Rader, 1977, as cited in Rapaport & Burkhart, 1984, p. 216).

  Christie and Geis's (1970) assertion that the manipulative Machiavellian demonstrates no gross pathologies seems based mainly on the premise that "neurotics and psychotics" lack sufficient reality perception to transact their deceits. This is, perhaps, a limited view of psychopathology and ignores the fact that delusions and hallucinations represent only part of the problems associated with mental disorders. Certainly, many of the Axis II disorders detailed in the *DSM IV* (1994) are demonstrative of maladaptive behaviors and cognitive processes, but not of delusional or hallucinatory perceptions (which are more typical of Axis I disorders).

However, Christie and Geis's argument does mesh with the previously mentioned feminist authors' assertions (Brownmiller, 1975; Koss, 1997; Koss, 1982; Messerschmidt, 1993; Scully, 1990). That is, the sexually aggressive male is best viewed as an occupant of some range of points along a continuum of accepted "normal" behavior that creeps into sexually aggressive behavior at some definite but not always discernible threshold. This would be in contrast to the earlier, traditional view of sexual aggressors as extreme, pathological rarities.

Ultimately, the distinction between pathological and non-pathological models of sexual aggression is not the focus of the current study, despite the importance of at least mentioning it here. The point is that Machiavellianism and narcissism serve as measurable dimensions of personality, whether they are considered to be of sufficient magnitude to be labeled as pathological or not. Determining the point at which the characteristics and behaviors of narcissism and Machiavellianism cross the line into clinical pathology is outside the scope of this study.

Christie and Geis (1970) developed their scale items by reading (and rereading) Machiavelli and comparing his works to other "power theorists." They noted that "unlike most power theorists, Machiavelli had a tendency to specify his underlying assumptions" about human nature (p. 8). This undoubtedly assisted them in their task. These authors analyzed *The Prince* and *Discourses* for concrete, specific assertions that could be developed into scale items. The initial result was a 71 item instrument with statements such as "A white lie is often a good thing" (p. 11); "It is safest to assume that all people have a vicious streak and it will come out when they are given a chance" (p. 11), and "The most important thing in life is winning" (p. 13). The items were administered in a Likert format. Several of the items were reverse-scored.

Some of the early findings about Machiavellianism bear directly on this study and consequently are discussed below.

Aspects of Machiavellianism

Bogart, Geis, Levy, and Zimbardo (1970) explored Festinger's (1957) theory of cognitive dissonance within the context of Machiavellianism. The researchers sought to investigate the theoretical principle that an individual could engage in a dissonant activity if he or she was a member of an "attractive group" (Bogart et al, p. 237) that condoned or encouraged the dissonant act. The prediction was that the subject would violate his or her own values and beliefs at the behest of an attractive group, because the subject wanted to emulate the members of that group. The subject would therefore cognitively justify the dissonant act. However, the researchers were also interested in the effect of an unattractive group on an individual's likelihood to engage in a dissonant action. Bogart et al. (1970) contended that engagement in such an act, if it occurred, might be explained by a private shift of cognition to support and rationalize the dissonant action.

The findings indicated several points. Overall, the high Machs tended to refuse to cheat when paired with a high-dissonance (unattractive) partner, but did cheat when the partner was low-dissonance (attractive). That is, high Machs engaged in cheating activity based on their ideas about their accomplice, not on their own moral principles. In contrast, low Machs' cheating activities were not related to how their partner was labeled. Bogart et al. (1970) proposed that high Machs acted on a cognitive label affixed to their partner, and low Machs were influenced by their personal involvement with the confederate.

The authors also found that high Machs were more detached from their own behaviors. Whether or not they engaged in cheating, their core attitudinal positions remained unchanged. This underscored the pragmatic tendencies that characterize Machiavellians (Bogart et al., 1970).

The researchers further reported that high Machs rely on cognitions to guide their behavior, but do not take prior actions into account in constructing subsequent cognitions. The authors noted, "a high Mach who disagrees with the item, 'Honesty is the best policy in all cases,' is not thereby endorsing the principle of dishonesty in all cases" (p. 255).

Machiavellians tend to conduct a rough risk-analysis before engaging in dissonant behavior. In the Bogart et al. (1970) study, high Machs cheated more with the low-dissonance or attractive partners. The authors contended that this indicates that Machiavellian individuals will engage in risky behavior with others if they perceive their accomplices to be resourceful and capable. They will cheat not as a gesture of camaraderie (as low Machs did), but only if they decide that it is tactically sound (Bogart et al., 1970).

Recall Boeringer's (1996) study on collegiate fraternity membership, athletics and their bearing on reported proclivity toward the use of coercion to attain sex in a no- penalty situation. In that work, Boeringer reported that fraternity members were more likely to use intoxicants and nonphysical coercion to obtain sexual gratification than were non-fraternity members. Boeringer also recounted that athletes were more likely to report that they would employ physical coercion for sexual gratification if they were assured of getting away with it (Boeringer, 1996).

Viewing these findings within the context of the conclusions reached by Bogart et al. (1970), one might discern two Machiavellian dynamics at work. The first relates to the idea of corroborating with, or modeling the behavior of peers who are perceived as competent. Fraternity members and athletes who engage in ritualistic initiations, study, socialize, endure difficulties, reside, and engage in other cohesive activities together will likely develop an affinity for their fellow members. This might well lead, via social comparison processes, to the ideation of peers as Bogart, et al's "attractive, high-prestige partner" (p. 253), reported as a condition for the high Mach individual to model deviant activity.

For example, a freshly initiated fraternity member or a rookie collegiate football player may witness fraternity brothers or teammates engage in sexually coercive behavior (implicit or physical) against women at a house party. Furthermore, he may well observe high prestige members of his group (say the fraternity president or the starting nose tackle) brag of their coerced sexual conquests. If the individual was a high Mach, he might model such behavior, even in the absence of other internal structures that may predict sexual aggression (such as dominance motive or hostility toward women [Malamuth et al., 1993]). This finding might demonstrate the viability of the role of Machiavellianism in sexual aggression, one that is not theoretically linked to other previously explored belief structures such as dominance, hostility toward women, and others.

The second Machiavellian dynamic that may be recognized from the Boeringer (1996) study is that of the reported findings based on the "no-penalty" condition attached to the scenarios. In that study, male athletes were more likely to report that they would employ force to gain sex if they were assured of getting away with it. These findings represent the high Mach tendency to rely on a rough risk analysis before engaging in questionable behavior.

Consider also the previously reviewed studies on social context, fraternity membership and sexual aggression (Boeringer et al., 1991; Schwarz & Nogrady, 1996). One of the main thrusts of the findings was the possibility that sexually aggressive conduct may not be predicted by the membership per se. Rather, the research suggests that other social comparison processes may play a role, processes that transcend the simple fact of fraternity membership.

Perhaps the Machiavellianism research can provide illumination here. If one considers Machiavellian tendencies as a social learning variable, an explanatory method of social comparison may emerge that sharpens the focus beyond membership/non-membership of a particular group. That is, the high Mach male must first determine the attractiveness of his models/accomplices before engaging in the risky behavior of sexual aggression. It is not the membership in a social group that determines social comparison. It is how that membership is perceived, similar to some of the points Wood (1989) described in her discussion of surrounding dimensions.

If social membership alone is an insufficient condition for males to commit sexual coercion, one may question on what the behavior does depend. Machiavellianism can provide some insight here. Against the template of Machiavellianism, one can perhaps discern a new mechanism of comparison. High Machs who perceive their deviant peers as competent might be more inclined to engage in the same activity themselves. The behavior could well hinge on the individual's perception of his peers, and not merely on the social contextual ties represented by those peers.

Wood (1989) detailed the importance of self-enhancement in an individual's comparison process: people engage in social comparison to view themselves in a positive light. Conversely, Bogart et al. (1970) asserted that high Machs assign little value to internally anchored self-concepts in their behavior. Instead, they make decisions based on risk assessments of external perceptions, with little regard for self-enhancement. Their decisions are based on gaining tactical advantage in interpersonal exchanges, not in elevating their personal sense of self-worth. However, it is argued here that for the high Mach, gaining a tactical advantage is indeed a self-enhancement, and that the Mach's self-worth is tied to winning life's little battles. As Kelly (1963), Lewin

(1997), and Allport (1958) purport, these cognitive structures have a degree of flexibility. It is consistent with Wood's (1989) assessment to conclude that high Machs are malleable in their social comparisons and resultant behavior. At the same time, it is reasonable to argue that the high Mach's decision-making processes are linked to a relatively stable cognitive mechanism, one that stresses personal gratification, safely achieved.

The Rapaport and Burkhart (1984) study reviewed above found that the strongest attitudinal predictors of sexual coercion were linked to those that measured the participants' attitudes that related to legitimizing aggression within a specific social context. They wrote that sexually coercive males perceive females as agents of opposition, a high Mach perspective. Furthermore, the low responsibility and socialization scores associated with sexual aggression have (at least) an intuitive relationship with certain tenets of Machiavellianism: the dearth of affect in interpersonal relations; the lack of interest in conventional morality; and, the low investment in ideological commitment. This last point is another possible link between Machiavellianism and sexual aggression: Low commitment to ideologies might translate to low commitment to women as people of worth and value, and could be manifested as a comparatively low grade of sexual aggression (such as promiscuity). This is speculative, of course, but could merit further study at a later date.

Grams and Rogers (1990) found that high Machs tend to use certain techniques for exerting interpersonal influence. These authors investigated how high and low Machs attempted to influence a research confederate in low, intermediate, and high motivation conditions based on business acquisition scenarios. Grams and Rogers reported that high Machs tended to use non-rational, indirect tactics of influence, including deceit and appeal to emotions, as well as attempting to instill a notion in the confederates' minds to comply with them. High Machs also tended to employ flattery and friendliness to gain affective influence over their targets.

Mudrack (1990) conducted a meta-analysis of twenty different studies of Machiavellianism and locus of control (LOC). He investigated studies that considered whether Machiavellians perceived their lives as governed by external forces, or if they felt in control of their own destinies. Using meta-analytic techniques, Mudrack determined an overall correlation of .38 between Machiavellianism and external LOC. Because of the statistically conservative method (and a confidence interval that contained no zero point) used by Mudrack, he considered this correlation to be significant.

This finding might seem counterintuitive given the Mach's excessive self-interest. One might intuit that the Mach has an internal LOC to account for the overwhelming self-interest that characterizes the Mach. However, Mudrack reasonably argues that the Mach engages in deceit, ingratiation and interpersonal manipulation in response to a perceived hostile world. The Mach relies on surface, readily attainable personal responses in reaction to controlling external forces. These manipulative tactics are favored over more internally seated traits, such as a work ethic (Mudrack, 1990). These conclusions are consistent with the studies discussed above that found an association between perceived peer activity and self-reported sexual aggression (Schwartz & Nogrady, 1996). Wood's (1989) model of social comparisons also fit well with Mudrack's conclusions: The high Mach demonstrates a contextual self-serving bias in his or her perceptions of the world.

Note the importance, too, of cognitive construction in Mudrack's (1990) conclusion. The Machiavellian perceives the world as a controlling, perhaps threatening place. The cognitive process responds with what has worked in the past: manipulation, deceit and non-rational appeal to emotion. The Mach has learned to deal with external events by reading them and employing the strategy that best fits the situation. This is essentially how cognitive schemas normally work, but the high Mach might well be operating at a more superficial level. That is, it could be speculated that the Machiavellian's cognitive style is to deal with a seemingly hostile world on a shallow cognitive level, with little deep internal processing.

Therefore, the high Mach displays characteristics of low social conscience, manipulation, excessive self-interest, low empathy, exploitiveness, deceitfulness, a desire for power and control, and perception of others as hostile. The sexual aggressor shares these belief structures of the high Mach. Furthermore, the tendency of the high Mach to engage in quick and shallow, short-term advantage-seeking behavior is also consistent with sexual aggression. Importantly, the high Mach's characteristics are particularly suited to explain much of the sexual aggression that is non-physically coercive; i.e., the use of deceit or verbal coercion to attain sex. This is of particular interest because of the high prevalence of acquaintance rape and intoxicant-induced rape (Rubenzahl, 1998; Schwartz, 1999).

NARCISSISM

Narcissism is the other personality dimension measured in this study for its association with sexual aggression. There are key elements in the sexual aggression studies that relate to narcissism, just as there are with Machiavellianism. The narcissist has feelings of "entitlement," is exploitive of others, is excessively self-absorbed, and has low empathy for others, among other components. In light of the sexual aggression literature reviewed above, narcissism should be tested as an associative or causal agent of sexual aggression. The Kosson and Kelly (1997) study reviewed earlier found some support for the significance of narcissism in non-physical sexual aggression in a series of multidimensional scales. Hurlbert and Apt (1991) reported that abusive husbands (not necessarily sexually abusive) displayed some characteristics of narcissism. However, narcissism has not been adequately explored as a factor in sexual aggression. This section reviews the definition and characteristics of narcissism, and then discusses its application to the current study.

Narcissism as a Clinical Disorder

Narcissism exists as a clinical personality disorder in the *DSM IV* (1994), and as such reflects a medical-pathological model of aberrant behavior. However, narcissism can and should also be regarded as a non-pathological personality construct.

Masterson (1981) wrote,

> The term "narcissism" has recently become so linked with one form of psychopathology that it is often overlooked that a normally developed or healthy narcissism, one definition of which is the libidinal investment of the self, is vital to a healthy adaptation. (p. 3).

Whether or not the magnitude of narcissism is such that the individual is determined to be pathological, the characteristics are the same: grandiose self-perceptions, low interest in or empathy for others, and excessive self-involvement (Masterson, 1981). While Masterson's work is essentially a clinical work (with case studies and a theoretical integration with the borderline personality), some of his observations pertaining to narcissistic personality types are worthy of mention here. For example, Masterson details the history of one patient who failed to differentiate between self and object-representation, that is, the realization that the world exists separately from the individual. Masterson wrote,

> The fantasy persists that the world is his oyster and revolves about him. In order to protect this illusion, he must seal off by avoidance, denial and devaluation those perceptions of reality that do not fit or resonate with the narcissistic, grandiose self-projection...
> (p. 13).

In general, the narcissist's cognitive style is such that he or she perceives the world in such a manner that the self-schema is of paramount importance, and that external events are to be either accepted or discarded according to their value in bolstering that schema. (It could well be that maladaptive schemas are more rigid and rash in their assimilation/accommodation criteria, although that question lies outside the scope of the current study).

It is interesting to note that, while Masterson was writing from a clinical perspective, and not from a social psychological one, one can still recognize the elements of schema-based cognitions in his work. The elements remain the same: the narcissist's perception that the world is there to serve him or her; that the self is the most important entity and takes precedence over all and that the self-schema must be nourished, regardless of consequences to others.

Non-clinical Aspects of Narcissism

Emmons (1987) noted the emergence of three dominant trends pertaining to the study of narcissism. The first such trend has focused on narcissism as a cultural or societal phenomenon. Emmons pointed out that society has become increasingly self-seeking and egoistic, citing the popularity of contemporaneous self-oriented books as an example.

The second trend noted by Emmons (1987) is the non-clinical, social psychological aspect of narcissism, with the biases and self-serving cognitions that were discussed earlier. This trend is demonstrated by people's (not just narcissists') tendency to take credit for successful outcomes and avoid responsibility for failed ones; to seek out information that will only fortify the existing schema, to view one's own actions by the situation and to view others' actions as generalized, stereotype behaviors.

Apt and Hurlbert (1995) identified and detailed the phenomenon of *sexual narcissism*. These authors asserted that sexual narcissism is essentially an intimacy disorder, marked by low self-esteem, an inability to give or receive emotional intimacy, and maladaptive beliefs about human relationships. Other examples of research addressing non-pathological narcissism include investigation into satisfaction (Kopelman & Mullins, 1992), adolescent personality correlates (Kerr, Patton, Lapan & Hills, 1994), and self-esteem and parental nurturance (Watson & Hickman, 1995). This non-pathological perspective of narcissism is the one most appropriate for the current study.

The third trend identified by Emmons (1987) is the clinical or pathological aspect of narcissism, as discussed above. This aspect has been extensively investigated in the past as a personality disorder, and is outside the scope of this study, except as a means to understand the underpinnings of the dimensional, non-clinical perspective of narcissism.

The current study will involve non-clinical participants, but this literature review draws from all three perspectives of narcissism identified by Emmons (1987). As stated above, this work relies on the clinical framework of narcissism. But it depends just as heavily upon the notion of narcissism as a personality dimension that is socially learned and manifests itself in individual actions as well as the United States culture.

There is support for viewing narcissism as a dimensional continuum of personality (Emmons, 1987; Watson and Hickman, 1995). Most attention has been devoted to extreme cases or manifestations, but the dimensional perspective is more useful to the current study than is the notion of the presence or absence of a particular pathology.

Narcissism and the DSM IV

While this work's perspective of narcissism is not bound by the clinical/pathological perspective, it would be helpful to review the criteria for Narcissistic Personality Disorder (NPD) as outlined by the *DSM IV* (1994). Such a review will enable better understanding of this phenomenon as a clinical disorder and as a personality dimension.

This manual described NPD as marked by "a pervasive pattern of grandiosity, need for admiration, and lack of empathy" (p. 658). Furthermore, the *DSM IV* reported that individuals with NPD are hypersensitive to narcissistic "'injury'" (p. 659). That is, rejection or criticism has a disproportionate impact on them, and they are prone to reactions of rage, disdain, or defiance. The disorder is characterized by fragile self-esteem, impaired interpersonal relations, feelings of entitlement, a hunger for admiration, a lack of empathy, and an assumption that others are entirely concerned about the narcissist's well-being. The individual with NPD is arrogant, disdainful and condescending.

The *DSM IV* outlines the following diagnostic criteria for the Narcissistic Personality Disorder:

> 1. has a grandiose sense of self-importance (e.g., exaggerates achievements and talents, expects to be recognized as superior without commensurate achievements);
> 2. is preoccupied with fantasies of unlimited success, power, brilliance, beauty, or ideal love;
> 3. believes that he or she is "special" and unique and can only be understood by, or should associate with, other special or high-status people (or institutions);
> 4. requires excessive admiration;
> 5. has a sense of *entitlement* (emphasis added), i.e., unreasonable expectations of especially favorable treatment or automatic compliance with his or her expectations;
> 6. is interpersonally exploitative, i.e., takes advantage of others to achieve his or her own ends;

7.   lacks empathy: is unwilling to recognize or
identify with the feelings and needs of others;
8.   is often envious of others or believes that
others are envious of him or her;
9. shows arrogant, haughty behaviors or
attitudes (p. 661).

These criteria are offered to display the clinical characteristics of
the narcissistic personality disorder, and to provide a foundation for the
discussion of narcissism as a non-clinical personality dimension.

Narcissism and Aggression

While identifying more extreme cases, the studies discussed below
establish the link between narcissism and aggression, an important
connection to make if this dimension is expected to be associated with
sexual violence. It is noted too that compensatory fantasy seems to play
a role in the level of violence.

Schulte and Hall (1994) pointed out that the narcissist's
precarious balance of self-perception as a good and adequate person
requires frequent external self-validation. When this need is frustrated,
the individual experiences a self-righteous fury and might act in an
aggressive manner (Kohut, 1972). Narcissists feel an overwhelming
need to punish and seek revenge for perceived slights in order to restore
their grandiose self-integrity. This tendency towards rage and punishing
behavior could be the driving force behind the terrible violence that
characterizes some rapes and sexual homicides. Narcissistic injury
could be one of the "triggering factors" discussed by Ressler, Burgess
and Douglas (1992):

> This man kept giving orders to the woman, thus
> indicating his fantasy for how he intended the sexual
> assault to proceed. Her lack of 'cooperation'
> shattered his fantasy. He became enraged and killed
> her. Another murderer recalled the triggering factor
> of the victim's trying to escape, although he did not
> recall the murder itself. His fantasy had centered
> around control and dominance; the victim's resisting

behavior made him murder to preserve his fantasy (p. 51).

Schlesinger (1998) seems to concur. He conducted a case study that examined the relationship between serial homicide and narcissism, and specifically mentioned the role of compensatory fantasy. In this case study, the subject, who was guilty of murdering two women, demonstrated the role of homicidal fantasy through the extensive planning of his crimes. Schlesinger argued that the narcissist faces an irresistible desire to preserve a powerful and controlling self-concept. This assertion is backed by Joubert (1998), who reported significant correlation between narcissism and Need for Power. Furthermore, Schlesinger (1998) noted the specific dimensions of narcissism that relate to serial homicide, including the roles of rigid or weak cognitions that can lead to sexual aggression. Schlesinger also noted the aggressor's indulgence in grandiose fantasies that are meant to compensate for sexual inadequacies, and the linkage of these to the perception of women as hostile creatures that inflicted narcissistic injury and rejection in the past. Note too the shades of Machiavellianism in these schemas of perceiving others (in this case women) as adversaries representing a hostile world.

Power Rape and Narcissism

Groth (1979) detailed the characteristics of a type of rape known as *power rape*. This is a form of rape typified by the need of the offender to exert dominance and possession over the victim. Groth (1979) wrote, "Sexuality becomes a means of compensating for underlying feelings of inadequacy" (p. 25). The power rapist seeks to attain control and mastery over the victim and will use any force he believes necessary to achieve sexual conquest. This type of offender also perceives the rape as a "test of his competency" (1979, p. 26). The power rapist frequently denies that the rape was forcible. He engages in the fantasy that the victim wanted to be raped and enjoyed the assault. Such rapists have been known to insist, after the assault, that they buy the victim a dinner or drink or ask to see the victim again. One of Groth's (1979) subjects, a power rapist, related: "Sometimes, after we'd have sex (i.e. after he raped the victim) I'd give the girl my telephone number, but none ever called. I guess they figured I didn't give them the right number" (p. 42).

The arrogance in this assertion is towering, and can be directly related the narcissistic tendencies of power rapists. This type of sexual aggressor also might ask the victim if she enjoyed the experience, or ask her if she would kiss him before he releases her, and in general demonstrates that he requires the admiration denoted in the *DSM IV* criteria. Many victims of rape might acquiesce to this need for admiration in order to survive the encounter. This only sustains and encourages the narcissist's quest for validation. There have even been instances in which the victim agreed to a second "date" with the rapist, to which she brought police personnel for surveillance and arrest of the offender, and the rapist still rationalized the experience. In these instances the offender maintained that the victim claimed rape only to protect her reputation (Groth, 1979). It is clear that narcissistic tendencies act as a mechanism to disengage the aggressor from rational introspection and to blindly rationalize their actions, even in the face of contrary evidence. While most people engage in some form of rationalization for their own embarrassing or shameful acts, narcissism seems to be especially suited to fostering this defensive reaction.

Although Groth (1979) did not include narcissism as a causative personality dimension in his rape research, his work on the power rapist draws a clear relationship between the construct of narcissism and sexual aggression. Note the bankrupt empathy set forth in the NPD inventory. This lack of empathy for others is a prime characteristic of sexual aggressors. Besides the sociopathic implications of non-empathy, one might reasonably relate lack of empathy to the objectification or dehumanization of others.

A comparison between the characteristics of the sexual offender known as the power rapist and the narcissist reveals a good prima facie consistency. It is contended that narcissism (or perhaps one of its measurable aspects) is an appropriate variable to examine in sexual aggression research (and perhaps other criminal acts as well). In particular, the coupling of narcissism with other personality dimensions, belief structures or disorders could prove to be a particularly fruitful path of research.

MACHIAVELLIANISM AND AGGRESSION

Studies examining the ssociation between Machiavellianism and narcissism are scarce. McHoskey (1995) compared these two personality systems and reported positive associations between Machiavellianism and the NPI dimensions of entitlement (.33), exploitativeness (.46) and exhibitionism (.27). McHoskey further reported an inverse association between Machiavellianism and the NPI dimension of self-sufficiency. This finding might seem counter-intuitive, considering the self-interested nature of the Machiavellian. However, McHoskey reports that self-sufficiency is an aspect of narcissism associated with the individual's adjustment, and suggests that this finding is more related to the Machiavellian's overall maladjustment than his or her self-interest. This finding might also be interpreted as reflective of the Mach's feelings of being controlled by external and hostile forces, as discussed earlier (Mudrack, 1990).

McHoskey (1995) stated that the main similarity between these two belief structures is the tendency to manipulate others. McHoskey also related the narcissistic characteristic of low empathy to the Machiavellian traits of affective detachment and task-orientation. He wrote, "both constructs...are associated with similar interpersonal features, e.g., dominance, arrogance, and lack of personal warmth" (p. 755).

ENTITLEMENT

In framing another cognitive model, it will be argued that entitlement stems from the concepts of Machiavellianism and narcissism, as discussed above by Christie and Geis (1970) and Raskin and Hall (1979), respectively. In short, the same cognitive structures that promote manipulation, non-empathy, and exploitation of others (among other components) also drive sexual aggression. This work purports that entitlement is also a dimension of these schemas, and may be theoretically derived from Machiavellianism and narcissism. It is believed that narcissism, Machiavellianism (and ultimately entitlement) converge to contribute to sexual aggression.

The potential importance of this research lies within the identification of the schematic dimensions that influence sexual violence. It has been established that cognitive schemas are learned, and it is contended that certain components of sexual aggression are also learned. This work proposes a cognitive structural approach toward identifying components of sexual aggression. More specifically, Machiavellianism, narcissism and ultimately entitlement are cognitive styles that may be associated with sexually aggressive behavior. If human behavior is determined in part by how individuals process and structure external influences, it is argued that a personality construct might be devised to explain certain activities, including sexual aggression.

This stance is not new; it could be likened to Sutherland's (1947) theory of differential associations and crime. Sutherland's work is valuable, indeed great, not because he introduced learning theory to criminal behavior (although this was a compelling achievement) but because he theorized that *cognitive events* are the central aspects in determining deviant or non-deviant behavior. That is, Sutherland went beyond simple modeling as a determinant of criminality, and conceptualized the notion of differential associations. These differential associations explained why all individuals who are exposed to similar social environments do not always behave similarly.

The values and definitions assigned to external events are part of the individual's social learning process, and can lead to criminal behavior, as theorized by Sutherland (1947). The deviant person learns criminal behaviors from intimate others and attaches values or definitions to these behaviors, depending on priority, frequency, duration and intensity. This process is at least partially a cognitive one, and may be perceived as reflecting the nature of schemas.

Entitlement, as proposed here, also represents a cognitive event, specifically as a series of cognitive events over time. This succession of events evolve into a particular belief structure about the self and the world. It is conceded that entitlement might already enjoy popularity as a component of criminal behavior: It has an intuitive appeal in popular culture and among laypersons for explaining bad acts. However, that does not preclude one from delving further into what drives entitlement, and from attempting to sketch out some of its operational constructs. Entitlement is merely introduced in the current work, and this study presents no direct data supporting its existence or nature. Even so, entitlement is a logical extension of established concepts, and it is not unreasonable to begin mapping out its dimensions.

Besides drawing from the elements of narcissism and Machiavellianism, entitlement is influenced by social construction, particularly the narrative constructions set forth by Gergen and Gergen (1988) and others who recognized the influence of cultural and storied icons on human behavior (Brownmiller, 1975). See Figure 1.

Figure 1. Entitlement model

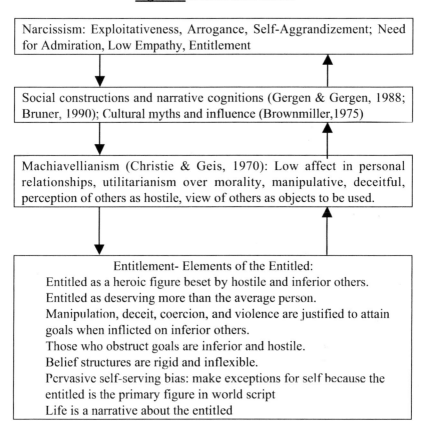

Narcissism: Exploitativeness, Arrogance, Self-Aggrandizement; Need for Admiration, Low Empathy, Entitlement

Social constructions and narrative cognitions (Gergen & Gergen, 1988; Bruner, 1990); Cultural myths and influence (Brownmiller, 1975)

Machiavellianism (Christie & Geis, 1970): Low affect in personal relationships, utilitarianism over morality, manipulative, deceitful, perception of others as hostile, view of others as objects to be used.

Entitlement- Elements of the Entitled:
Entitled as a heroic figure beset by hostile and inferior others.
Entitled as deserving more than the average person.
Manipulation, deceit, coercion, and violence are justified to attain goals when inflicted on inferior others.
Those who obstruct goals are inferior and hostile.
Belief structures are rigid and inflexible.
Pervasive self-serving bias: make exceptions for self because the entitled is the primary figure in world script
Life is a narrative about the entitled

CHAPTER 5

Methodology

SAMPLING

Sampling Plan

The sample plan for this study was a single-stage, stratified, proportionate cluster scheme. The resulting sample was one of randomly selected clusters (in this case undergraduate classes) and stratified across class level (the selected classes represent a progression from freshman to senior representation).

Although it may seem that freshman students would be over-represented because they made up two sampling quadrants of the frame (Figure 2), the percentage of selected freshmen was held as proportional to the population percentage. The freshmen participants were volunteers from two randomly drawn courses rather than one. The proportions were matched as closely to the university percentages as possible. While a perfect match was not possible, this method allowed greater representativeness for freshmen, who alternate in taking the two courses in question, English 101 and History I between semesters. That is, freshmen who take English 101 one semester take History I the following semester, and vice versa.

Because of the nature of this study, the sample consisted exclusively of males. The focus of this work is on male sexual aggression as a function of personality dimensions and socialization variables. While it is understood that there are sexually aggressive females, and that their behavior also merits research, females as aggressors are simply outside the scope of the current study. Furthermore, the relative frequency of female sexual violence is dramatically lower than for that of males, and the male sexual aggressor presents the greater social problem.

A target N of 300 students was used. This was based on considerations of method of analysis and intended generalizability to the undergraduate male population. Given the adage of 30 cases per independent variable (seven in this study), 300 exceeds the minimum N of 210 needed for regression. Expanding the N to 300 increased generalizability to the undergraduate males of this particular university and allowed for some general conclusions about this particular population. The increased N also resulted in more stable estimates (Weisburd, 1998).

The sample was composed of undergraduate male students at a mid-sized university in the Northeast. Babbie's (1998) admonitions against using availability samples were duly noted. While availability samples have been the accepted mode for much of the cited research, this study attempted to reduce sampling error through randomized cluster sampling and stratification of the sampling frame.

This study's sampling goal was to reasonably represent the male undergraduate students at the institution under study. While the findings of this study might not be statistically generalizable beyond the university site, the sampling plan for this study attempted to improve upon the availability samples used in other studies of this type. It is contended that the sample was well-constructed and yielded data that were sufficiently trustworthy to make solid decisions and insights about the research hypotheses. Similarly, an adequately constructed sample allows one to make at least preliminary insights about another, similar sample.

To initially organize the population, the sampling plan called for stratification across class level (freshman, sophomore, junior, and senior). The undergraduate population of the university campus in question was 11,375 (Office of Academic Resources). Of this population, 44.2%, or 5,032 are male. Residential students, that is, those who actually reside on the campus, make up 34.3% of the population ($n = 3900$). While this last detail was not included as a variable in this work, it provides a more complete picture of the particular university used in this study.

The population of this institution broke down by race as .7% Hispanic, 4.8% African-American, .2% Native American, .9 % Asian, and 90.8% Caucasian. Because minorities constituted such a small percentage of the study population, race and ethnicity were not addressed as variables, as any findings would be based on under-representation of these groups. Koss, Gidycz and Wisniewski (1987) reported a statistically significant effect for race/ethnicity, with 10% of African American men, 7% of Hispanic men, 4% of White men, and 2% of Asian men self-reporting rape. However, those authors cautioned that race and ethnicity might be confounded with regional variables, so those results should be viewed with some prudence.

Sampling Stages:
The sampling strategy employed was as follows. In the first stage of sampling, clusters of male students were sampled. For the first stage, the sampling frame consisted of all individual English 101 (freshmen), History I (freshmen), English II (sophomores), and Synthesis (juniors and seniors) class sections offered for the appropriate semester. This listing of classes made up a sampling frame stratified by collegiate class level. Next, the number of males needed from each strata was determined. The number of male students per class was estimated by multiplying the estimated class size by .44 (the proportion of males in the university population) to each class. At this point, simple division of the number of males needed at each grade level by the estimated number of males in each class determined the number of classes (clusters) that were needed from each stratum. The researcher over-sampled to compensate for non-participation. For the freshman stratum, half of the target freshman N were drawn from the History I and English 101 classes (Figure 2.)

Figure 2. Clusters of selected coursework stratified by class level to yield a sample N proportionate to the university population.

Freshman English	Freshman History
Individual classes selected randomly. Represent 36% of population. Target N of total sample= 300 Target N of Freshmen selected from Freshman English and History = 108 Actual N of freshman = 95	Individual classes selected randomly. Freshman samples were selected from both this class and the Freshman English class. Combined with Freshman English to constitute the freshman N of 95.
Sophomore English	**Synthesis Class (Juniors and Seniors)**
Randomly selected classes. Sophomores represent 20% of population. Target N of total sample= 300 Target N of sophomores= 60 Actual N of sophomores=70	Randomly selected classes. Jrs and Srs combine to represent 43% of population. Target N of total sample= 300 Target N of Jrs/Srs=129 Actual N of Jrs/Srs=140

As stated earlier, the researcher randomly selected the determined number of classes from each stratum. This generated a sampling frame for each collegiate class level. This frame consists of all elements (males) from all targeted courses per grade level.

Two waves of sampling were initially conducted in order to ensure an adequate sample size. A third wave of sampling was then employed to ensure adequate representation of upper level students. In this wave, colleges, disciplines and then individual upper level classes were randomly selected for participation.

Table 1 indicates the degree to which the sample proportions of class levels approximated the population parameters. As indicated by the table, the proportions of the final sample closely matched the targeted proportions for each class level.

Table 1

Comparison of Class Level Proportions for Sample and Population (N=308, 3 missing)

Class Level	Sample Number	Sample Proportion	Population Number	Population Proportion
Freshman	95	.31	1840	.36
Sophomore	70	.23	1015	.20
Junior/Senior	140	.45	2177	.43

Note. Proportions have been rounded and might not total 1.00.

Response Rate

Of the 116 professors ultimately approached, twenty-three scheduled survey dates their classes. The remaining professors either failed to respond or were unable to accommodate the research. Of the 308 students requested to participate, only one student declined. Professors who declined to offer participation were noted and their classes were eliminated from the sampling frame. No class or individual student participated more than once.

Once the individual classes were drawn, male participants were fully informed of the nature of this study. Participation was strictly voluntary. The professors of the classes played no role in selecting the students, and were not present during the data collection process.

INSTRUMENTS

The Sexual Experience Survey

The Sexual Experiences Survey (SES) (Koss & Oros, 1982) was administered as a measure of the dependent variable of sexual aggression. This instrument has been heavily employed in previous research (Boeringer, 1996; Koss & Gidycz, 1985; Koss, Gidycz, & Wisniewski, 1987; Koss & Gaines, 1993; Malamuth, Sockloskie, Koss & Tanaka, 1991; Malamuth, 1986; Malamuth, Heavey, & Linz, 1993; Rapaport & Burkhart, 1984; Scott, Madura, & Weaver, 1998; Meyer, Vivian, & O'Leary, 1998) to measure experiences that indicate a proclivity for sexually aggressive behavior. The SES is a 10-item instrument that asks study participants about past behaviors with varying levels of sexual aggressiveness (Appendix B). Each item refers to a particular level of sexual coercion, ranging from verbal pressure to the use of alcohol as a coercive tool to physical violence. The original survey asked dichotomous, *yes* or *no* questions about these activities, yielding a score from *0– 10*. However, in the current study, the index was modified to a Likert response format, ranging from *Never* to *Very Often.*

Koss and Gidycz (1985) assessed the Sexual Experience Survey scale with a population of 448 undergraduate students, 143 of whom were male (the population of interest in this work. These authors report an internal consistency (Cronbach's alpha) of .89 for males who took the inventory. Koss and Gidycz also conducted a test-retest reliability assessment and reported a mean item agreement of 93% between the two scale administrations. The Pearson product-moment correlation between males' self-reported sexual aggression and their scale responses was .61 ($p < .001$) (Koss & Gidycz, 1985). These coefficients may be viewed as appropriate for the current study. In addition, the instrument appears to be a reliable and valid method of inquiry into the stated hypotheses.

However, the SES has faced criticism for its purported ambiguity (Gilbert, 1998). Gilbert focused especially on the operationalization of intoxicant-induced coercion reflected in item 8, which reads "Have you had sexual intercourse with a woman who didn't want to because you gave her alcohol or drugs?" Gilbert was referring to the female version of the index, which addresses the respondent as a potential victim rather than as a potential perpetrator. For example, the female version worded the same item as "Have you had sexual intercourse when you didn't want to because a man gave you alcohol or drugs?" Regardless, his criticism deserves consideration, and will be further explored in a later section of this work that discusses content validity of all the instruments used in this study.

Other items from this survey include statements such as:

> "Have you engaged in sex play (fondling, kissing, or petting, but not intercourse) with a woman who didn't want to because you overwhelmed her with continual arguments and pressure?"

> "Have you had sexual intercourse with a woman who did not want to by threatening or using some degree of force (twisting her arm, holding her down, etc) to make her?" (Koss, Gidycz & Wisniewski, 1987).

These items were measured as ordinal level data on a Likert-type scale with five response categories that ranged from *Never* to *Very Often*.

The Narcissism Personality Inventory

The independent variable was measured using the Narcissism Personality Inventory (NPI) (Raskin & Hall, 1979). The NPI is a 40-item scale that indicates a general score for narcissism, with seven component scales for Authority, Exhibitionism, Superiority, Entitlement, Exploitativeness, Self-sufficiency, and Vanity (Appendix C). The NPI scoring key reported a reliability alpha score of .84 for males.

Like the other instruments employed in this study, the NPI is a well-established scale and has been used extensively in past studies (see Lambourn & Day, 1995; McHoskey, 1996; Irwin, 1995; Cramer, 1996; Rhodewalt & Morf, 1995; Gabriel, Critelli & Ee, 1994; Watson & Biderman, 1993; Shulman & Ferguson, 1988; Mullins & Kopelman, 1988). The scale items are paired statements, to which the respondent indicates the one with which he most agrees. The scale yields a narcissism score that serves as an interval level of variable. Examples of NPI items are:

> A. I find it easy to manipulate people
> B. I don't like it when I find myself manipulating people;
>
> A. I insist on getting the respect that is due me.
> B. I usually get the respect I deserve (Raskin & Hall, 1979).

The Machiavellianism Scale

The Machiavellianism Scale (Mach IV) (Christie & Geis, 1970) is a Likert-response format instrument based upon the writings of the famed royal advisor and power theorist Niccolo Machiavelli. Christie and Geis reported a split-half reliability coefficient of .79. Gable and Dangello (1994) also reported an alpha of .79 for the Mach IV; other authors report that the Mach IV reliability has consistently been found to be at least .70 in various test-retest and split half tests (Watson, Biderman & Sawrie, 1994). The Machiavellian scales have been used extensively in past research as personality measures (Cherulnik, Way, Ames & Hutto, 1982; Moore, Okanes & Murray, 1982; Turner & Martinez, 1977; Ward & Katz, 1998; White, 1993).

The scale itself consists of 20 statements about human nature and abstract morality to which the respondent indicates the degree to which he or she agrees or disagrees. The following are examples of the items found on the Mach IV scale:

> "Honesty is the best policy in all cases."
>
> "The best way to handle people is to tell them what they want to hear" (Christie & Geis, 1970, p. 17).

This scale was in five-increment Likert format for this study. Several of the items are reverse-scored in this instrument to control for habituated response patterns.

OTHER INDEPENDENT VARIABLES

As discussed in the previous chapters, narcissism and Machiavellianism are personality dimensions that have been linked to social processes that include social comparison, social construction and cultural conditioning of the sexually aggressive male. Therefore, these processes should be investigated to determine their relationship, if any, with sexual aggression. Given the premise that males learn attitudes toward women over time and within the contexts of social, male-dominated groups, five additional independent variables are analyzed in the current study. They are fraternity membership, athletic participation, age, self-reported estimate of sexual experience compared to peers, and collegiate class level (freshman, sophomore, junior or senior).

Fraternity Membership and Athletic Participation

Fraternity membership was included in an attempt to gain insight into whether the social processes of male groups are associated with sexual aggression (a question which has been addressed in the past, but with no clear pattern of results).

The association between athletic participation and sexual aggression has also been addressed in the literature, as reviewed above. However, like fraternity membership, the relationship between the two variables remains unclear. This study intended to determine if narcissism or Machiavellianism might exist as underlying variables that transcend mere membership in particular groups as predictors of sexual aggression. That is, if fraternity or athletic membership was found to be associated with sexual aggression, the accompanying Mach and narcissism scores may be inspected to determine if they are similarly associated. This would allow researchers to look beyond mere membership in these social groups and perhaps give some direction in investigating more complex, dimensional factors of sexual violence.

Age

The respondents were asked to provide their age in years. This variable might suggest influences of general life experience that are independent of other collegiate social or opportunity variables, such as class level or membership in fraternities or participation in athletics.

Earned Credits

Earned credits provide a ratio level measurement of class level. Analysis of the relationship between class level and sexual aggression could provide some insight as to whether any of the collegiate social processes have an effect over time. Class level served as a general measure of socialization in the college environment. It was assumed that, if there are observed differences in the variables of sexual aggression, narcissism or Machiavellianism across class levels, it would be possible to hypothesize about these dimensions and behaviors as they relate to the socialization of the student over a period of time. This might generate useful and important future research. To collect ratio level data appropriate for regression analysis, this question was asked as "at the end of this current semester, how many credits will you have earned?"

Self-reported Sexual Experience

Malamuth, Heavey and Linz (1993) suggested that promiscuous sexual activity among certain men might be an indicator of sexual aggression. Respondents were asked to estimate their level of sexual experience, as compared to their peers, on a 10-centimeter magnitude estimation response format. This format provided interval level data and was intended to indicate past opportunity to engage in sexual aggression.

Linear and multiple regressions were used to analyze the relationships between these variables. These are discussed below in the analysis section. However, it should be pointed out here that, to allow multiple regression analysis, athletic participation and fraternity membership were dummy coded (0 = no membership/participation; 1 = membership/participation). Athletic participation was operationalized as non-intramural, collegiate level sports.

DATA COLLECTION PROCEDURES

Administration of the Scales

The instruments were group-administered to males in the selected classes. Access was gained via an introductory letter to the appropriate professors and the tester explained the study and the nature of informed consent.

The associates who assisted in the data collection were two male Ph.D. criminology students who had successfully completed a required ethics course as well as at least two doctoral level research classes. These associates read the research proposal and were trained by the researcher in how to administer the surveys and answer any questions that the participants might have.

Tester Effect

The possibility of a tester effect was a potential concern. All three of the survey administrators were Caucasian males within the same rough age range. The greetings, explanation of the study and the informed consent form were scripted to ensure uniformity of administration. Still, it was deemed necessary to check the results for any significant variation between the administrators. A tester effect was checked for by comparing the mean sexual aggression scores among the three administrators. No such tester effect was found.

CHAPTER 6
Analysis and Results

ANALYSIS PLAN

An analytical plan was devised in order to summarize the procedural steps in interpreting the results. This plan outlined the steps in two phases (1) the reliability and validity of the measures and (2) the statistical analysis of the data.

Reliability Analysis of the Instruments

A reliability analysis of the Mach IV, NPI and SAS instruments was conducted in order to assess the internal consistency of the items. For the Mach IV and NPI, internal consistency was determined by the coefficient alpha. These are scales (as opposed to indices) because they are intended to measure a single underlying construct (Machiavellianism and narcissism) and one would expect a strong inter-item correlation, if the instruments measured the phenomena they were constructed to measure (DeVellis, 1991). The reliability of the SAS was assessed by arranging the items, based on level of progressive violence, into a Guttman model, for which a coefficient of reproducibility was calculated.

The reliability analyses were then used to make decisions about the internal consistency of the instruments, and to determine whether there were items that for whatever reason might be best excluded to improve the instrument's homogeneity. These reasons might include obsolete wording or references, ambiguous syntax (to include sexist language), or tenuous connection to the underlying construct. In this way the instruments could be "cleaned" and their effectiveness maximized.

Reliability Analysis of the Machiavellianism IV Scale:
An initial internal consistency analysis of the Mach IV scale was conducted. The resulting coefficient alpha of .56 was considered weak, and the individual items were inspected to determine if their exclusion would more fully reflect the construct. However, merely raising the alpha value was only one consideration in deciding which items should be excluded. Blanket rejection of any item with a poor item-total correlation, simply to elevate the alpha value, ignores important validity concerns. There were some low-correlation items that were nevertheless judged to represent the underlying construct of Machiavellianism so quintessentially that they were retained.

An example of this is item 6, which states, "It is safest to assume that all people have a vicious streak and it will come out when they are given a chance." (Like every item on the Mach IV scale, the respondent could indicate his reaction to the statement in a five increment Likert format, ranging from *strongly disagree* to *strongly agree*). While this item's item-total correlation was only .16, it was retained because the item deeply taps the core of Machiavellian cynicism toward others and vigilant risk-analysis.

Taking into account both the correlative magnitude and the content validity, four items were eliminated from the Mach IV scale for this analysis.

Justifications for Elimination of Mach IV Items:
Items 16, 17, 18 and 20 were ultimately deleted from the scale. Item 16 stated "Most people forget more easily the death of their father than the loss of their property." This item's correlation was .00 and its deletion immediately raised the alpha from .56 to .57. Moreover, it was deemed a stilted and peculiar statement that at least some respondents might have found confusing.

Item 17, "Most people who get ahead in the world lead clean, moral lives," appears to squarely hit the underlying construct. However, the correlation score was a weak .10. Upon reflection, it was decided that although at first glance this item appeared to be a reasonable measure of Machiavellian cynicism toward others, the culture of the mid to late 1990s might have socialized many of the respondents to simply accept a degree of immorality from high profile figures. In consideration of the highly publicized moral and legal difficulties of the nation's elected officials and administrators, as well as the equally publicized crimes (let alone immoralities) committed by professional athletes, musicians, actors, and other celebrities, it is not surprising that this item had low association with the construct of Machiavellianism. An individual so socialized might simply believe that most people who "get ahead in the world" (considered as celebrities or political leaders) tend towards moral bankruptcy, while still holding no other Machiavellian beliefs. The issue of whether this is the fault of the affected high profile individuals themselves, or of media excesses, will not be debated here. The point is, heavy and ongoing cultural influence, as manifested by media reports of crimes and immoralities conducted by celebrities and politicians ("those who get ahead in the world") could lead a low Mach respondent to conclude that this is a reasonable statement, without harboring any other Machiavellian beliefs.

If this speculation had any merit, one would expect a high mean score for this item. Low as well as high Machs alike would agree that those who get ahead in society tend to lack morals, which would drive up the mean score for item 17. In fact, this item scored the highest mean on the scale ($\overline{X} = 3.8$). This indicates that one need not be Machiavellian oneself to recognize the well-publicized ethical lapses of high profile figures. Deletion of this item raised the alpha score from .57 to .62.

Item 18 was "Generally speaking, people won't work hard unless they are forced to." This item's correlation was a feeble .10. Moreover, it does not appear to have overriding content validity. While the item does address the Machiavellian aspect of cynicism toward others, it does not seem to sufficiently tap the core essence of manipulation and self-servingness associated with this construct. Eliminating item 18 raised the alpha from .62 to .68

Item 20 reads, "Most men are brave." The item-total correlation was a paltry .05. The high Mach response would be a flat disagreement to this statement, reflecting a Machiavellian low view of human nature. However, this item contains sexist language, and it is unclear as to whether it is asking whether the respondent believes that most people are brave, or if just men are. Therefore, this item could be tapping attitudes about the superiority of men over women, rather than addressing Machiavelli's (1513/1981) original warning that "men" in general are "anxious to flee danger" (p. 60). For this reason, coupled with the low item-total correlation, item 20 was stricken from the analysis. Deleting this item raised the final alpha base score to .69.

Inspection of the remaining items revealed that their content validity was satisfactory. The modified scale had a variance of 45.78 and a standard deviation of 6.77, compared to the original variance of 71.78 and standard deviation of 8.47. A relatively high degree of variance is desirable in a scale because it indicates the instrument's ability to discriminate among individual respondents' differing levels of the construct under investigation. However, a lowered variance might be expected when dropping unreliable items (DeVellis, 1991). While the new alpha does not quite meet the .70 level suggested as a general guideline suggested by Nunnally (1978, cited in Spector, 1992) it was the best that could be done with this scale for this sample. Inspection of the corrected item-total analysis revealed that the alpha score could be raised no further from the deletion of additional items.

Reliability Analysis of the Narcissistic Personality Inventory:
A reliability analysis of the NPI was conducted. The alpha score was .84, corroborating the .84 reported by Raskin and Hall (1979). The item-total correlations ranged from .08 (item 22–"I sometimes depend on people to get things done/I rarely depend on anyone else to get things done") to .52 (item 12–"I like having authority over other people/I don't mind following orders"). Item 22 was inspected for validity concerns, and it was decided to retain the item despite the low score, as it squarely tapped the self-sufficiency aspect of narcissism. The reliability analysis for the NPI resulted in a variance of 48.10 and a standard deviation of 6.94.

Reliability Analysis of the Sexual Experiences/Aggression Survey:
Koss and Gidycz (1985) reported an internal consistency alpha of .89 for male participants. A reliability analysis for this sample resulted in an alpha score of .76.

Inspection of this index suggested that the items could be rank-ordered into a format of increasing violence or coercion. It was then decided to treat the re-ordered index as a Guttman instrument, so that it could be examined to determine if the frequency of aggressive responses decreased as the items progressed in violence. In this way, a coefficient of reproducibility could be calculated via the formula:

Coefficient of reproducibility = 1 − (total errors/number of scale items x N)

This would provide another measure of the instrument's reliability, but to do so the items would need to be ordered into a Guttmann format.

Guttmann scale items tap incremental increases of a particular attribute, in this case, sexual aggression. Affirmation of any item on a Guttman scale indicates sanction of all prior items (Devellis, 1991). The Koss and Oros (1982) survey used in this study measures progressive dimensions of sexual aggression (sex play, intercourse, other sex acts) and assesses levels of coercion used (verbal pressure, authority over victim, intoxicants, threatened or attempted violence). However, it does not progress in a hierarchical, Guttmann-style ordering of items (nor is there any reason to believe that the survey's authors intended it to do so). The index does lend itself to this type of ordering, however, and it provides another method of assessing the instrument's reliability for the purposes of the current study.

In re-ordering the SAS/SES items, it was decided that the level of violence or coercion used against the victim was the most salient aspect of the construct. It was anticipated that the re-ordering would result in decreasing frequency of responses as the level of reported violence increased. For example, it was surmised that more subjects would report using verbal pressure to kiss and fondle a woman than would report committing anal rape through physical force, to use an extreme case.

However, the progression of the items seemed to more readily reflect increasing levels of sexual access (such as penetration as opposed to fondling) than violence (such as holding the victim down as opposed to using chemical coercions). For example, it was expected that more respondents would report the use of alcohol or drugs to coerce sexual intercourse (item 8) than would report using physical force (twisting arm, holding down, threatening harm) to coerce sexual play (item 3). Item 3 implies more physical violence even though the level of sexual access is heightened in item 8.

Finally, items which asked about sexual coercion associated with positions of authority (2 and 7) were ordered higher than the level of violence alone might suggest, on the assumption that the respondents in this sample, being undergraduate students, would have had less opportunity to sexually aggress in this fashion.

In making the re-ordering decision, this researcher consulted with two Ph.D. sociologists, a registered psychiatric nurse experienced in working with sexual offenders, a sexual offender therapist, a Ph.D. criminology candidate, a graduate sociology student and the director of a center devoted to assisting victims of rape and domestic violence.

Their advice varied, but after review of their responses, the items were re-ordered thusly (the number reflects the original placement of the item in the SES):

> 1. Have you ever had a woman give in to sex play (fondling, kissing, or petting, but not intercourse) when she didn't want to because you overwhelmed her with continual arguments and pressure?

> 5. Have you attempted sexual intercourse with a woman (getting on top of her, attempting to insert your penis) when she didn't want to by giving her alcohol or drugs, but intercourse did *not* occur? (emphasis original).

> 2. Have you had sex play (fondling, kissing, or petting, but not intercourse) with a woman who didn't want to because you used your position of authority (boss, teacher, camp counselor, supervisor) to make her?

> 6. Have you had sexual intercourse with a woman when she didn't want to because you overwhelmed her with continual arguments and pressure?

> 8. Have you had sexual intercourse with a woman who didn't want to because you gave her alcohol or drugs?

> 7. Have you had sexual intercourse with a woman who didn't want to because you used your position of

authority (boss, teacher, camp counselor, supervisor) to make her?

3. Have you had sex play (fondling, kissing, or petting, but not intercourse) with a woman who didn't want to because you threatened or used some degree of physical force (twisting her arm, holding her down, etc.) to make her?

4. Have you attempted sexual intercourse with a woman (getting on top of her, attempting to insert your penis) when she didn't want to by threatening or using some degree of force (twisting her arm, holding her down, etc.) but intercourse did *not* occur? (emphasis original).

9. Have you had sexual intercourse with a woman when she didn't want to by threatening or using some degree of force (twisting her arm, holding her down, etc.) to make her?

10. Have you had sex acts (anal or oral intercourse or penetration by objects other than the penis) with a woman who didn't want to because you threatened or used some degree of physical force (twisting her arm, holding her down, etc.) to make her?

After the items were re-ordered, the number of errors was calculated for each item. Errors were considered responses that endorsed higher level items but did not affirm all preceding items. A coefficient of reproducibility of .97 was calculated. This was a remarkably high measure and indicated that highly aggressive subjects also tend to commit lower acts of aggression as well. The coefficient of reproducibility is essentially a measure of reliability, in that an individual who scores a certain level of aggression would be expected to reproduce the score in other instances. This coefficient also serves as an indirect validity check, in that it tends to validate the construct of sexual aggression as a construct that exists in incremental stages of magnitude, and that these progressive stages can be reliably measured.

Content Validity of the Instruments

Content validity of the instruments was determined through comparison
of items with the domain measures of behaviors, established in the
literature, as representative of the specific construct under
investigation. The content of the items was inspected to gauge the
degree to which they reflected the domain. DeVellis (1991) cautions
that assessing content validity in scales measuring subtle constructs
such as attitudes and beliefs can be difficult, as there is no specified
"universe of items" (p. 44) from which to theoretically draw a sample.

Content Validity of the Machiavellian IV Scale:
In assessing the content validity of the Mach IV scale, the elements of
the Machiavellian personality as defined by Christie and Geis (1970)
were compared both to individual scale items as well as the culmination
of the entire scale. Furthermore, Machiavelli's original writings in *The
Prince* (1513/1981) were examined for comparison with the instrument
and with Christie and Geis' theoretical derivations. Finally, the
literature review of Machiavellianism was considered. In conducting
this evaluation, every attempt was made to maintain the underlying
theoretical premise that "a scale has content validity when its items are
a randomly chosen subset of the universe of appropriate items"
(DeVellis, 1991, pp. 43-44).

From the above sources, a matrix describing the dimension of
Machiavellianism and its representation in the scale can be constructed
(Table 2). As indicated on the table, there was one element of
Machiavellianism, derived from *The Prince* (1513/1981), that could
have been added to more fully represent the construct. The notion that a
reputation for cruelty held certain advantages for the prince was a
recurring theme in Machiavelli's work, and was added here to add to
the construct's "universe of appropriate items" (DeVellis, 1991, pp. 43-
44). This is not intended to denigrate Christie and Geis's (1970) scale
but only reflects the attempt to assess content validity for this particular
study. This is especially so given the potential application of a
reputation for cruelty component could have with the matter under
study.

Table 2

Content Validity Assessment for the Machiavellianism IV Scale

Elements of Machiavellianism	Corresponding scale items
Manipulation/Deceit	1, 2, 5, 7, 10, 15
Opportunism and advantage-seeking	1, 4, 9
Lack of affect toward others	3, 6, 11, 15
Lack of conventional morality	5, 8, 10, 13, 15, 17
Excessive utilitarianism	4, 7, 9, 12
Distrustful of others	3, 6, 14, 17, 18, 19, 20
Perception that a reputation for cruelty has advantages	Not addressed

Overall, the Machiavellianism IV scale appears to have good content validity. However, the Machiavellian theme that having a reputation for cruelty is advantageous is not addressed in the scale.

Content Validity of the Narcissistic Personality Inventory:
Raskin and Hall (1979) report seven domains for the NPI: Authority, Exhibitionism, Superiority, Entitlement, Exploitativeness, Self-Sufficiency, and Vanity. Furthermore, they report the corresponding item numbers for each domain, or component of Narcissism (Table 3). The NPI also demonstrates good content validity for the various domains.

Table 3

Content Validity for the Narcissistic Personality Inventory (NPI)

Domain	Corresponding Items
Authority	1, 8, 10, 11, 12, 32, 33, 36
Exhibitionism	2, 3, 7, 20, 28, 30, 38
Superiority	4, 9, 26, 37, 40
Entitlement	5, 14, 18, 24, 25, 27
Exploitativeness	6, 13, 16, 23, 35
Self-Sufficiency	17, 21, 22, 31, 34, 39
Vanity	15, 19, 29

Note. This table is adapted from NPI material supplied by the Tulsa Institute of Behavioral Sciences and Dr. Raskin. Used with permission.

Content Validity for the Sexual Experiences/Aggression Survey:
This index has undergone criticism for validity issues. Gilbert (1998) charged that the operational definitions of rape and attempted rape in two items of the instrument were subject to misinterpretation by respondents. Gilbert's criticism was aimed at the female version of the survey, which differs from the male version used in the current study only in the phrasing of the questions. The female version is aimed at asking women about the extent of their victimization. The male version asks about the extent of the respondents' victimizing behaviors. However, the same validity threat exists regardless of which version is used.

Specifically, Gilbert took issue with the two items that deal with the use of intoxicants as coercive tools:

> Item 5: "Have you attempted sexual intercourse with a woman (getting on top of her, attempting to insert your penis) when she didn't want to by giving her alcohol or drugs, but intercourse did *not* occur?" (emphasis original).

Item 8: "Have you had sexual intercourse with a woman who didn't want to because you gave her alcohol or drugs?"

Gilbert (1998) argued that an affirmative response to these items did not signify whether any force (or threat thereof), duress or intentional incapacitation was used. It is unclear, Gilbert maintained, whether this meant that the woman exchanged sex for drugs or alcohol or had her inhibitions sufficiently diminished to engage in a sexual act she later rued. On the male version, there is the question as to whether the man used alcohol or drugs to gain a consent that he recognized as reluctant, but that he considered as consent nonetheless. This ambiguity calls into question whether or not these items meet the legal standard for attempted rape or rape.

Similarly, it could be questioned whether item 5 addresses intentional incapacitation of the victim, which is an essential element of using coercive intoxicants in a rape. The item begs the question, if intoxicants were used as disabling level of force, what prevented the intercourse from occurring? If it was an attack of conscience, does this item still measure attempted rape, or something else?

Three of the independent raters mentioned above whom examined the scale for ordering of progressive violence also questioned these two items on the same grounds. Despite these concerns, the item was retained as worded. It was decided that modifying the wording to explicitly address intentional incapacitation would dilute the construct of sexual aggression as a continuum of behaviors shared by aggressive and non-aggressive men. Using alcohol to wear down a woman's will and gain sexual access may or may not meet the legal standard of rape, but it is a more aggressive act than leaving her alone after she has said no. The item does include the wording "when she didn't want to," so the male respondent is aware that he had to overcome resistance. In the male version, a positive response indicates knowledge on the aggressor's part that the act involved some level of coercion. This is not true of the female version criticized by Gilbert (1998), which leaves some doubt as to whether the experience was the result of ambivalence, miscommunication, or later regrets. In light of this, all items on the SAS/SES were retained.

Construct Validity of the NPI and Mach IV Scales:

The NPI and Mach IV scales were analyzed to compare similar domain measures. Shared domains relating to self-serving tendencies, manipulation, superiority, exploitation of others, and entitled attitudes were correlated. The modified Mach IV scale was correlated with the NPI components of Superiority, Entitlement and Exploitativeness. Inspection of Pearson's *r* scores revealed several significant positive correlations. Additionally, a reliability analysis was conducted among these items, yielding an alpha of .73 among the 31 items. This demonstrates that the two constructs are correlated in key aspects of self-servingness, and is consistent with earlier findings reported by McHoskey (1995).

SUMMARY OF RESULTS

Review of Research Questions

Before the analysis and results are presented in detail, a general overview of the findings and their relationship to the research questions is given here. To review, the research questions addressed in this study were:

1. Is there an association between narcissism and sexual aggression among males?

2. Are Machiavellianism and narcissism among males correlated with each other?

3. Is there an association between Machiavellianism and sexual aggression among males?

4. Are there other personal or demographic variables that are associated with sexual aggression among males, (i.e. sexual experience, age, class level, fraternal and athletic membership)?

Overview of Results

Of the 299 participants who completed the sexual aggression survey (9 had missing values) in this study, 110 (36.8%) reported at least some level of sexual aggression. In general, the results indicated that both narcissism and Machiavellianism share significant associations with sexual aggression. *T*-tests demonstrated that those subjects scoring highly in self-reported sexual aggression also tended to have higher scores in these belief structures (significant at the .05 level). However, bivariate and multiple regression analyses revealed that they were not satisfactory explanatory variables for sexual aggression. That is, while most high-aggressives tended to be high Machs and narcissists, many low aggressors also had high scores in these constructs.

The same relationship held true for self-reported sexual experience. While this variable did not explain a significant proportion of variance in sexual aggression, those who reported higher levels of sexual aggression tended to also report higher scores in sexual experience, as demonstrated by *t*-tests. Fraternity membership, athletic participation, class level (as determined by number of earned credits), and age bore little relationship with sexual aggression.

FREQUENCIES AND DESCRIPTIVE STATISTICS

Frequencies and descriptive statistics are reported here to provide an initial, overall picture of the results. The means, standard deviations and *n* for each variable are reported in Table 4.

It should be noted that the mean Machiavellianism score reflects the modified 16-item Mach IV scale discussed above, and is not suitable for comparison to scores reported in related studies, as it would tend to be lower. The NPI mean of 17.25 is comparable to the mean of 16.50 for males reported by Raskin (2001). The SAS/SES mean was 1.06 under the modified Likert format.

Table 4

Descriptive Statistics for All Variables (N=308)

Variable	Valid n	Mean	Standard Deviation
Age	308	20.77	2.49
Sex Exp	308	5.90	2.45
Mach Score	303	46.43[a]	6.77
NPI Score	292	17.25	7.11
Sex Agg Score	299	1.06	.26
Credits Earned	305	56.30	38.63

Note. a. Mach scale was modified to a 16-item format.

Mean scores do not properly represent the dichotomous variables (athletic participation and fraternity membership), as they were coded only as *0* for non-participation or *1* for participation. Therefore, frequencies of affirmative responses are presented in Table 5 to more meaningfully represent the presence of athletes and fraternity members in the samples.

As shown below in Table 5, 13.6% (*n* = 41) of the respondents were student athletes and 17.9% (*n* = 55) were fraternity members. Six respondents reported being both athletes and fraternity members.

Correlations

The Pearson product-moment correlation coefficient was computed to identify the extent of the linear relationship existing between the independent variable and sexual aggression (Table 6). This correlation furnishes information about the directionality and strength of the correlation between the two variables. Pearson's *r* provided an estimate of the relationship between the two measures through a comparison of

Table 5

Frequencies for Athletic Participants, Fraternity Members (N = 308)

Variable	Score	Frequency	Valid Percent
Athletic	.00[a]	267	86.4
	1.00[b]	41	13.6
Fraternity	.00[a]	253	82.1
	1.00[b]	55	17.9
Athletes and Fraternity members		6	1.9

Note. a. Indicates non-membership/participation; b. indicates membership/participation

Table 6

Pearson r Correlations for All Variables

Variable	SexAgg	NPI	Mach	SexExp	Frat	Athletic	Age	Credits
SexAgg	1.00	.14*	.15*	.18*	.10	-.02	.18*	.09
NPI	--	1.00	.24**	.26**	.12*	-.01	-.12*	-.10
Mach	--	--	1.00	.21**	.00	-.03	-.04	.01
Sex Exp	--	--	--	1.00	.08	.06	.04	.09
Frat	--	--	--	--	1.00	-.04	-.04	.01
Athletic	--	--	--	--	--	1.00	-.07	-.05
Age	--	--	--	--	--	--	1.00	.58**
Credits	--	--	--	--	--	--	--	1.00

Note. *. Correlation is significant at the .05 level (2-tailed).
   **. Correlation is significant at the .01 level (2-tailed).

**. Correlation is significant at the .01 level (2-tailed).

Machiavellianism and sexual aggression *(r* = .15); narcissism and sexual aggression (*r* = .14); self-reported sexual experience and sexual aggression (*r* =.18); and age and sexual aggression (*r* = .18). However, these results reveal little about the relationship between the variables other than it is a positive, linear one. The correlation between Machiavellianism and narcissism also indicates a positive, linear relationship, but the *r* is not considered high enough to raise multicollinearity concerns about the scales. Multicollinearity is undesirable because it tends to make the slope estimates and the partial correlation coefficients oversensitive to sampling and measurement errors. Therefore, the use of highly correlated independent variables necessitates highly accurate measurements and large sample sizes. While one might strive to meet these criteria regardless, multicollinearity increases the risks that there will be large differences from one sample to the next (Blalock, 1979).

Fraternity membership, athletic participation, and earned credits have such weak Pearson r scores that they do not demonstrate any relationship at all with sexual aggression. Initial inspection of these findings would indicate general agreement with results reported by Koss and Gaines (1993) and Schwarz and Nogrady (1996). These issues are addressed in the discussion chapter.

Another noteworthy result is that the associations both narcissism and Machiavellianism have with self-reported sexual experience (*r* =.26 and *r* = .21, respectively) is greater than that which they have with sexual aggression (*r* = .14 and *r* = .15, respectively). This finding is also explored further in the discussion section.

SEXUAL AGGRESSION

Table 7 displays selected frequencies and descriptive statistics for scores on the SES/SAS to present a general overview of the results. One finding of note is that while most respondents (63.2%) reported that they had never used any form of sexual coercion, including verbal pressure to engage in sex play (the lowest level of aggression), a significant percentage (36.8%) did report using some level of coercion in the past.

Table 7

Frequencies for Sexual Aggression Scores (N = 299, 9 missing)

Variable	Score	Frequency	Valid Percent	Cumulative Percent
Sex Agg	.00	189	63.2	63.2
	1.00	43	14.4	77.6
	2.00	31	10.4	88.0
	3.00	8	2.7	90.6
	4.00	8	2.7	93.3
	5.00	3	1.0	94.3
	6.00	7	2.3	96.7
	7.00	4	1.3	98.0
	8.00	1	.3	98.3
	9.00	1	.3	98.7
	10.00	2	.7	99.3
	>10.00	2	.7	100.0

Note. The Sexual Experiences/Sexual Aggression Survey was originally developed by Koss and Oros (1982). The SES/SAS used in this study used a differing response format, ranging from *never* to *often*, resulting in higher scores than would be expected from the original *yes* or *no* format.

Table 8 displays the frequency of positive responses to the individual SAS/SES items. The SAS/SES used in this study was modified to a continuous response format, from *never* to *very often*. However, this table reflects only whether a given response was positive or negative. If a participant in this study responded positively to any item, this was counted as an affirmative response regardless of whether the respondent reported the behavior as frequent or rare. Therefore, an *often* response was counted the same as a *rarely*, that is, as *yes*. This reduction of the data level allows comparison with other studies in which the original response format (*yes* or *no*) was employed. In this way, percentages of rape, attempted rape, and other levels of sexual violence could be reported in the reduced format used by other studies that used the original SES/SAS. This modification allowed greater sensitivity of measure.

Table 8

Frequencies of Positive Responses for Sexual Aggression Survey Items (N=308)

Item	n	Frequency of Positive Responses	Valid Percent
SAS 1	302	102	33.77
SAS 2	303	18	5.94
SAS 3	303	8	2.64
SAS 4[a]	302	7	2.32
SAS 5	303	27	8.91
SAS 6	303	28	9.24
SAS 7	303	5	1.65
SAS 8[b]	303	12	3.96
SAS 9[b]	303	2	.66
SAS 10[b]	301	1	.33

Note. The Sexual Experiences/Sexual Aggression Survey was modified for this study to allow responses from *never* to *very often.* However, for the purposes of this table, the scores are reported as yes or *no* to allow comparison with other studies. Superscript *a* indicates attempted rape, *b* indicates rape.

Narcissism and Sexual Aggression

Comparison of Means and t-Tests:
T-tests are used to determine statistical significance of the difference of means between two groups. The *t*-tests were employed here to compare high and low narcissists in their mean sexual aggression scores. Quartiles for the narcissism scores were computed. The top quartile of narcissism scores was identified as high narcissist (NPI scores >= 22). Similarly, the bottom quartile was computed and these subjects were deemed as low narcissists (NPI scores <=12). *T*-tests were then

conducted on the mean sexual aggression scores for the high and low narcissists to determine the significance of the difference between the groups.

As shown below in Table 9, there was a statistically significant difference in the mean sexual aggression scores between the upper and lower quartile narcissists. This indicates that sexual aggressors tend to be more narcissistic than non-aggressors. However, the *t*-test does not explain or predict sexual aggression. Inspection of the scatter plot indicates that although aggressors tend to score higher on the NPI, many high narcissists are also non-aggressive. This finding suggests that while sexual aggressors tend to be more narcissistic than do non-aggressors, narcissism alone does not reliably predict sexual violence. It is likely that narcissism manifests itself in a variety of ways, many of which are unrelated to sexual aggression.

Table 9

T-test of Significance Between Low and High Narcissists for Sexual Aggression Scores (Top and Bottom Quartiles)

	N	Mean SAS Score	SD	t score
High Narcs	80	1.31	2.24	
Low Narcs	73	.33	.71	3.56*

*Significant at the .05 level

It was then decided to investigate whether these findings would hold up with a different division point between high and low narcissists, one that did not eliminate 52% of the sample. Therefore, the narcissist scores were again divided into high and low narcs, but this time the division was made at the mean narcissism score 17.25. Respondents with scores less than or equal to 17 were identified as low narcs; those with scores greater than or equal to 18 were considered high narcissists. As Table 10 depicts, the significance of the means between the two groups held up in this *t*-test as well.

Table 10

T-test of Significance Between Low and High Narcissists for Sexual Aggression Scores (Mean Cutpoint) (N=288, 20 missing)

	N	Mean SAS Score	SD	t score
High Narcs	142	1.42	2.81	
Low Narcs	146	.74	1.40	2.60*

*Significant at the .05 level

Bivariate Regression for Narcissism and Sexual Aggression

Linear regression was conducted to determine the r^2, and the standardized beta weights were inspected for strength of association. Next, a confidence interval was computed and interpreted. This procedure was used for each independent variable. The standardized beta weights, r^2 coefficients, and confidence intervals were inspected to see if they contained a zero. The results of the bivariate regression analysis for narcissism and sexual aggression are summarized in Table 11.

Table 11

Coefficients and Confidence Intervals for Narcissism and Sexual Aggression (N=284, 24 missing)

Independent Variable	Unstandardized Slope	r^2	95% Confidence Interval for B	
			Lower	Upper
Narcissism	.04	.03	.01	.08

Narcissism explained a mere 3.0% of the variance in sexual aggression. For every unit increase in narcissism, sexual aggression was increased by .04 units on the ten-item scale.

Inspection of Slope Coefficients for Narcissism and Sexual Aggression

Linear regression permitted the construction of the slope coefficient b. The coefficient b (also referred to as the regression weight or the slope) represents the average change in Y that is associated with a one-unit change in X. In the bivariate regressions, the unstandardized slope was inspected to determine the impact of the independent variable on the dependent one.

Confidence Intervals for Narcissism and Sexual Aggression

The confidence interval for the narcissism slope contained no zero and is not overly wide (.01 - .08), therefore the interval is significant. However, the lower endpoint is precariously close to zero, and the upper bound is not much higher. The practical significance of this interval is doubtful.

Machiavellianism and Sexual Aggression

Comparison of Means and t-tests:
The highest and lowest quartiles were determined for the Machiavellian scores, as they were for the narcissism scores. Mach scores of 51 or above were considered as high Machs, and individuals who scored 42 or below were considered low Machs. There was a statistically significant difference in mean SAS scores between high and low Machs, but as on the narcissism t-test, one cannot assess the predictive value of this independent variables from this result. Inspection of the scatter plot for these variables indicates a tendency toward high Machiavellianism among sexual aggressors, but also shows a substantial number of high Machs who are non-aggressive. Still it is clear that high Machs are significantly more aggressive than are low aggressors. Table 12 below depicts this relationship.

Table 12

T-test of Significance Between Low and High Machs for Sexual
Aggression Scores (Top and Bottom Quartiles)

	N	Mean SAS Score	SD	t score
High Machs	74	1.50	2.47	
Low Machs	77	.75	1.61	2.21*

*Significant at the .05 level

Table 13

T-test of Significance Between Low and High Machs for Sexual
Aggression Scores (Mean Cutpoint) (N=295, 13 missing)

	N	Mean SAS Score	SD	t score
High Machs	143	1.41	2.67	
Low Machs	152	.68	1.56	2.8*

*Significant at the .05 level

Like narcissism, Machiavellianism appears to be an attendant
construct of sexual aggression, in that sexual aggressors tend to be high
Machs. However, because many high Machs are non-aggressive, this
personality structure does not explain or predict sexual aggression, as is
demonstrated by the regression analysis discussed next. As was noted
in narcissism, there are probably many possible manifestations of
Machiavellianism, of which sexual aggression is only one.

Like with the narcissism variable, it was then decided to cut the
high and low Machs at the mean Mach score of 46.43 (High Machs >=
47; Low Mach <= 46). Again, this enabled a comparison test that does
not ignore half of the sample. Table 13 demonstrates that the significant
difference between the mean SES/SAS scores for high and low Machs
remained.

High and Low Aggressors and their Mach and Narc scores:
If Machiavellianism and narcissism are presumed to be accompanying conditions of sexual aggression, it would be worthwhile to know if there was a significant difference in the scores of these variables among the highest and lowest sexual aggressors. If Machiavellianism and narcissism is related to sexual aggression in this way, does it follow that the most highly sexually aggressive men have significantly greater Mach and narc scores than those who scored in the mean or lower on the SES/SAS? That is, does the magnitude of the Mach or narcissism structure correspond to the level of sexual aggression?

To test this, the highest aggressors (defined as those scoring 8 or above on SES/SAS) were compared with those scoring at the mean ($\overline{X}$ = 1.06, or 1.00) or lower on the SAS. The results are displayed in Table 14.

Table 14

T-tests of Significance Between Highest and Mean-Low Aggressors for Mach and Narc Scores

	Mach t	Narcissism t
Highest aggressors (SAS>=8)		
	3.17*	1.92
Mean and low aggressors (SAS<=1)		

*Significant at the .05 level

Table 14 demonstrates that of the two variables, the magnitude of Machiavellianism appears to bear some relationship with the magnitude of sexual aggression, whereas this relationship does not occur with narcissism. It is imprudent to assign too much weight to these findings however, as the *n* for the highest aggressors is so low (*n*=6). Nevertheless, this issue might be further investigated in future research if an appropriate number of high aggressors can be identified

Table 15

Coefficients and Confidence Intervals for Machiavellianism and Sexual Aggression (N=293, 15 missing)

Independent Variable	Unstandardized Slope	r^2	95% Confidence Lower	Interval B Upper
Machiavellianism	.04	.02	.01	.07

Bivariate Regression for Machiavellianism and Sexual Aggression:
Table 15 displays the coefficients and confidence intervals for Machiavellianism and sexual aggression. The unstandardized beta weight is .04, indicating an increase of .04 in sexual aggression for every unit increase in Machiavellianism, as measured on the 16-item scale. The r^2 is .02, meaning that 2.3% of the variance in sexual aggression is explained by Machiavellianism. The confidence interval around the slope for this variable contains no zero and indicates some significance for this result, although both endpoints are very close to zero. This casts doubt on the practical significance of the slope of this factor.

Self-reported Sexual Experience and Sexual Aggression
Self-reported sexual experience was measured by participant's response on a ten- centimeter line. This variable was included in the study to provide a rough estimate of past opportunities to engage in sexual aggression, as well as to represent the participant's sexual acquisitiveness. As with narcissism and Machiavellianism, *t*-tests comparing the mean SAS/SES scores between upper and lower quartile sexual experience scores demonstrated a statistically significant difference between the two groups. See Table 16.

Table 16

T-test of Significance Between Low and High Self-Reported Sexual Experience for Sexual Aggression Scores (Top and Bottom Quartiles)

	N	Mean SAS Score	SD	t score
High Sex Exp	78	1.58	2.49	
Low Sex Exp	78	.58	2.61	2.45*

*Significant at the .05 level

As with the narcissism and Machiavellianism variables, a second *t*-test was run with the high and low sexual experience scores divided at the mean Sexual Experience score (mean score = 5.90). High sexual experience scores were identified as those greater than or equal to 6.0. Low sexual experience scores were identified as those that were less than or equal to 5.9. As with the narcissism and Machiavellianism variables, sexual experience retained its significant association with sexual aggression. See Table 17 below.

Table 17

T-test of Significance Between Low and High Self-Reported Sexual Experience for Sexual Aggression Scores (Mean Cutpoint)

	N	Mean SAS Score	SD	t score
High Sex Exp	164	1.35	2.28	
Low Sex Exp	135	.71	2.20	2.45*

*Significant at the .05 level.

In the regression run, the unstandardized beta weight indicates that for every one-unit increase of sexual experience, sexual aggression increased by .17 units. Sexual experience accounted for 5.6% of the variance of sexual aggression. See Table 18.

Table 18

Coefficients and Confidence Intervals for Self-Reported Sexual Experience and Sexual Aggression (N=298)

Independent Variable	Unstandardized Slope	r^2	95% B Confidence Interval Lower	Upper
Sex Exp	.17	.06	.10	.28

The confidence interval contains no zero and is therefore significant. While the endpoints are still low, this positive relationship lends support to the notion that sexual promiscuity might be associated with sexual violence, at least among some men, as proposed by Malamuth, Heavey and Linz (1993).

Age and Sexual Aggression

Age in years explained 3.2% of the variance in sexual aggression. Every unit increase in age indicates a mean increase of .16 in sexual aggression. The confidence interval contains no zero so the slope for this variable is statistically significant. See Table 19.

Table 19

Coefficients and Confidence Intervals for Age and Sexual Aggression (N=299)

Independent Variable	Unstandardized Slope	r^2	95% B Confidence Interval Lower	Upper
Sex Exp	.16	.03	.06	.26

Fraternity Membership and Athletic Participation

Notably, neither fraternity membership nor athletic participation demonstrated any association with sexual aggression. This contradicts the findings of some past studies (Boeringer, 1996; Boeringer, Shehan & Akers, 1991; Crosset & Ptacek, 1996; Ward, Chapman, White & Williams, 1991) but is consistent with others (Koss & Gaines, 1993; Schwartz & DeKeseredy, 1997; Schwartz & Nogrady, 1996). There was no significant difference in the mean sexual aggression scores between fraternity members and non-fraternity members ($t = 1.24$). Nor did a t-test between athletes and non-athletes reveal any statistically significant difference ($t = .02$).

Fraternity membership accounted for one per cent of the variance in sexual aggression ($r^2 = .01$). The beta weight indicates a .10 increase in sexual aggression for every standardized unit increase in fraternity membership, but it should be noted that this and the athletic participation variable are dichotomous, and could only be scored as 0 or *1*. This confidence interval contains a zero and is rejected as insignificant. The t-tests also resulted in no significant difference between athletes and non-athletes for mean sexual aggression scores.

Athletic participation has a negative unstandardized beta weight of -.10. For every unit increase in the independent variable, sexual aggression might be expected to decrease in magnitude by .10 units. This is a dichotomous variable and was scored as a 0 or 1. Athletic participation explains zero variance in sexual aggression. The confidence interval contains zero. For this sample, athletic participation was an insignificant variable in explaining sexual aggression.

Earned Credits and Sexual Aggression

Earned credits was a non-significant variable in determining sexual aggression. The coefficient of determination shows that this independent variable explained only .30% of the variance of sexual aggression. The confidence interval contains zero and this slope has no significance.

Machiavellianism and Narcissism

As mentioned earlier, the NPI and Mach IV scales were analyzed to compare similar domain measures. The two constructs share domains relating to self-serving tendencies, manipulation, superiority, exploitation of others, and entitled attitudes. The modified Mach IV scale was correlated with the NPI components of Superiority, Entitlement and Exploitativeness. A Pearson's r of .211 was calculated, indicating significance at the .01 level (2-tailed).

Table 20

Correlation Between Machiavellianism and Narcissism (N=288)

	Mach	NPI
Mach	--	.21**
NPI	.21**	--

**Significant at the .01 level (two-tailed).

MULTIPLE REGRESSION ANALYSIS

Following the example of other, similar research employing two or more scales as independent variables for sexual aggression (e.g., Malamuth, Heavey & Linz, 1993; Rapaport & Burkhart, 1984) the data were analyzed via multiple regression.

Multivariate regression analysis provides a useful method of determining the proportionate contribution of each independent variable to the dependent variable of sexual aggression. Regression was an appropriate method given the levels of data and the premise that the dependent variable was the product of more than one cause (Lewis-Beck, 1980). Multiple regression offers a more complete explanation of the dependent variable, in that human behavior is rarely the outcome of a single cause. Multiple regression also allows, in part, a method for taking into account the interrelationships among the independent variables (Weisburd, 1998).

The residual, or error term accounted for other contributory factors related to sexual aggression that were not investigated here. The error term encompasses all of the other psychological, environmental, situational and other factors that contributed to an individual's past sexually aggressive actions.

In multiple regression, one is endeavoring to predict one dependent variable from a group of independent variables (Blalock, 1979). In the current study the dependent variable was sexual aggression and the independent variables were Machiavellianism, narcissism, fraternity membership, athletic participation, and class level. In this form of multivariate analysis, one defines the regression equation as "the path of the mean of the dependent variable Y for all combinations of X_1, X_2..., X_K....for every combination of fixed X's there will be a distribution of Y's (Blalock, 1979, p. 452). Blalock further related that if one assumed a multivariate normal population (one in which each variable is normally distributed around all of the others) then the following assumptions about regression will be met: that regression equations will be in the format written above; that the Y's will be normally distributed about the fixed X's and that there will be equal variances (homoscedasticity).

Multiple Regression Results

The relationships of Machiavellianism, narcissism, athletic participation, fraternity membership, age, overall level of sexual experience and class level are considered for their contribution to the explained variance.

As depicted in Table 21, the coefficient of determination ($r^2 = .090$) demonstrates that the independent variables combined to explain a mere 9% of the variance in sexual aggression, leaving 91% unexplained. The weak coefficient demonstrates that there are obviously other factors involved in predicting sexual aggression besides the attitudinal and social dimensions represented by the independent variables used in this study.

The strongest predictor of sexual aggression in this model is self-reported sexual experience, indicating perhaps the importance of opportunity in determining whether one is sexually aggressive or not. It could also indicate that certain belief structures that drive sexually acquisitive behaviors could also account for sexually aggressive behavior. This supports the sexual aggression model set forth by Malamuth, Heavey and Linz (1993), in which those authors proposed that sexual promiscuity could be relevant to sexual aggression among some males. However, the predictive value of sexual experience is still too low to allow for any real conclusions. See Table 21 below.

Table 21

Coefficients and Confidence Intervals for All Independent Variables and Sexual Aggression (N=277, 31 missing)

Independent Variables	Standardized Beta	$\underline{r}^2$	95% Confidence Interval-B Lower	Upper
		.09		
Sex Exp	.20		.06	.25
NPI	.10		-.01	.06
Mach	.10		-.01	.06
Age	.26		-.06	.21
Frat	.07		-.24	.91
Credits	-.02		-.01	.01
Athletic	-.02		-.41	.21

Machiavallianism (B = .10) and narcissism (B = .10), although found to have significant confidence intervals on individual regression runs, lost this significance in the multiple regression model. It is possible that these attitudinal and belief systems are too subtle and underlying to account for a measure of sexual aggression in this model.

However, since fraternal membership, athletic membership, and earned credits demonstrated such little association with sexual aggression, it was speculated that perhaps the rape-supportive, masculine peer culture was not limited to institutionalized organizations (Koss, 1996; Schwartz & DeKeseredy, 1997). If social comparisons and shared attitudes exist outside of athletic and fraternity organizations as well as within them, it would be reasonable to find no particular association between these variables and sexual coercion. A sexual aggression model that excluded these variables was therefore tested in order to get an indication of whether this fundamental notion held any merit (Table 22).

Table 22

Coefficients and Confidence Intervals for Selected Independent Variables and Sexual Aggression (N=277, 31 missing)

Independent Variables	Standardized Beta	r^2	95% Confidence Interval -B Lower	Upper
		.09		
Sex Exp	.10		-.02	.21
NPI	.11		.00	.08
Mach	.01		-.01	.07
Age	.21		.00	.08

Table 22 reflects negligible differences in the significance of the slope confidence levels and in the standardized Betas than the previous multiple regression model (Table 21). The confidence interval for the Sexual Experience slope now contains a zero, eliminating its predictive significance.

In the final wave of regression analysis, all variables *except* narcissism and Machiavellianism were run against the sexual aggression variable. This resulted in an r^2 of .06.

A run was then conducted with the addition of narcissism alone, resulting in an r^2 of .07. Finally, narcissism was withdrawn and replaced by Machiavellianism. The resulting r^2 was .08. See Table 23.

Table 23 indicates that Machiavellianism brings slightly greater PRE explanation to the run than does narcissism. However, when viewed within the context of the low overall r^2 and the relatively small PRE measures contributed by both of these variables, it is difficult to determine any real significance from this finding. Number of earned credits, athleticism and fraternity membership were all insignificant variables in this study. These findings and their implications are discussed in the final chapter.

Table 23

Separated PRE Measures of Narcissism and Machiavellianism and Coefficient of Determination

	r^2
All variables except Machiavellianism and narcissism	.06
All variables plus narcissism, without Machiavellianism	.07
All variables plus Machiavellianism, without narcissism	.08
All variables	.09

CHAPTER 7

Discussion and Conclusions: The Entitled Aggressor

GENERAL DISCUSSION

First, the low explanatory value of these variables in predicting self-reported sexual aggression should be addressed. Clearly, there is more contributing to this behavior than the few personality dimensions and socialization variables that were investigated in this work. Yet, the correlation analyses reveal that narcissism, Machiavellianism and level of sexual experience are positively associated with self-reported aggression. Those with higher Mach, narcissism and experience scores had (statistically) significantly higher mean sexual aggression scores. There were few high aggressors with low narcissism and Machiavellian scores; however, there were a substantial number of high narcs and Machs who reported low sexual aggression.

What are the theoretical implications of this? The most readily apparent one is that other variables are involved in the process that links belief systems or personality dimensions to overt sexually coercive behavior. Narcissism and Machiavellianism are not enough. Such possible predictors could comprise measures of hostility, anger, acceptance of violence, masculinity, or other like constructs. Future research that incorporates these variables could yield stronger predictive measures.

Additionally, investigation into macro-structural variables such as race, socioeconomic status, ethnicity, etc. may well add explanatory value to the problem of sexual aggression, especially if investigated alongside the personality dimensions studied here. Such a research plan could well provide useful insight to the problem of sexually aggressive behavior and heighten the current understanding of the problem.

However, too great an emphasis on structural factors tends to over-generalize men (or whatever group is under study) and ignores individual differences among their attitudes and behaviors. Criminal behavior is ultimately an individual act, and loading macro-variables into every criminological study ignores the role of individual personality correlations related to crime.

The current line of research is aimed at understanding the cognitive-personality makeup of the sexual aggressor, and this particular study does have a limited scope (as does any study). Certainly, any researcher could always measure more variables, and higher explained variance might be the reward. However, decisions need to be made as to research scope, both for administration manageability, and (more importantly) for theoretical use. If an imaginary research project could somehow measure every possible predictor of human behavior and result in 100% of explanation of variance, how useful would that result be in constructing a parsimonious and workable theory of whatever phenomenon is being studied?

Furthermore, this study had the usual limitations inherent in any research of this type, i.e. with a self-report instrument measuring criminal and sexual behavior. Although the sample was carefully selected to be representative of the university at which it was drawn, the results are generalizeable only to that particular institution, and no further.

The current work undertook its objective by measuring two personality dimensions and a few socialization variables, all of which were derived from past scholarship and which could be argued to have solid content validity as predictors of sexual aggression. Clearly, higher predictive value of the tested variables would have been desirable. However, that does not mean the correlative associations that were discerned are worthless. The relationships described in the results chapter do reveal some patterns of association that reasonably allow for discussion, with the caveat that further research is needed to establish viability for any kind of "entitlement" model.

DISCUSSION OF KEY VARIABLES

Narcissism and Sexual Aggression

Narcissism was a poor predictor of sexual aggression, but proved to be a strong attendant condition. Sexual aggressors tended to be more narcissistic than non-aggressors, but the factor explained little of the variance in the dependent variable. *T*-tests resulted in a statistically significant difference between the means of SAS/SES scores for high and low narcissists. Therefore, while sexual aggressors tend to be more narcissistic than non-aggressors, narcissism does not predict the variable, in that many narcissists also reported low sexual aggression scores. Sexual violence seems to be only one potential behavior in which narcissistic individuals might manifest that personality dimension.

It was expected that narcissism would bear some relation to sexual aggression. Narcissism is consistent with the characteristics of Groth's (1979) description of power rapist. According to Groth, the power rapist is one who uses sexual violence as a tool to exert dominance and possession over the victim. Furthermore, the power rapist often denies that his sexual conquest was forced, and fantasizes that the victim enjoyed the attack. This is consistent with the narcissistic function of grandiose self, which Svrakic (1990) describe as a brittle and defensive construct that demands successes (including imagined ones) from external reality. Svrakic also formulated the narcissist's value system as malformed, leading to a "constant search for grandiosity in any domain and at any cost" (1990, p. 190). This continuous seeking of gratification and perpetuation of false beliefs about themselves, their actions and their victims suggest a linkage between the power rapist and narcissism.

The power rapist's need to exert control and dominance over the victim, his tendency to give the victim orders or to ask her to evaluate his performance (reflecting a need for admiration), his use of denial to protect a brittle or fragile sense of self and the offender's bankrupt empathy all support a theoretical linkage between sexual aggression and narcissism. Therefore, the tendency of sexual aggressors to be more narcissistic than non-aggressors was expected.

However, narcissism explained very little variance in sexual aggression. This could be attributed to the different ways in which the narcissistic dimension of one's personality might be manifested. Schulte and Hall (1994) reported that clinical narcissists (those diagnosed with Narcissistic Personality Disorder) had a tendency to demonstrate violence in a self-righteous rage as a reaction to narcissistic injury. Schlesinger (1998) argued that sexual and serial murderers acted out behaviors associated with narcissism. However, these findings do not preclude manifestations of narcissism that have nothing to do with sexual aggression. Lasch (1979) and Miller (1997) have both elucidated the impact of narcissistic tendencies on modern culture in a variety of manifestations, in terms of values, identities, behaviors, and attitudes. Sexual aggression could well stand as one more outcome of individual and cultural narcissism among American males. There are other factors that mediate how narcissism is expressed that were not identified or measured in this study. This is an area that warrants further research attention in the future.

Self-Regard and Self-Esteem of the Aggressor:
The issue of positive self-regard and violence has been addressed before but remains an issue of contention. Martin (1985) reported that assaultive criminals tended to have an excessively positive self-concept. More recently, Baumeister (2001) suggested that aggressive criminals tend to have too much self-esteem, not too little, and that such individuals believe themselves to be "special, elite persons who deserve preferential treatment" (p. 99). Baumeister rightly points out that self-esteem and narcissism are not the same constructs. However, the magnitude of self-regard is a consistent element between the two. The NPI comprises domains of superiority, entitlement and vanity, all of which are consistent with inflated self-regard. Therefore, the results of this study indicate that inflated self-regard (as measured by the NPI) can be a strong attendant condition of sexually coercive behavior, and could well be associated with other forms of criminal violence.

Whether the narcissist actually has low self-esteem and acts in superior contemptuous, arrogant and even sadistic ways because of some compensatory mechanism that is shielding feelings of inferiority (Gilligan, 1996; Martin, 1985), or if certain criminals really are grandiose and harbor feelings of superiority (Baumeister, 2001) will not be settled here. It is noteworthy that narcissism is significantly associated with self-reported sexual aggression, although it does not explain it.

The sexually aggressive narcissist's arrogance leads him to target women and to consider them as objects that owe him admiration and adoration. When these are not forthcoming, the narcissist might become enraged (Kohut, 1972) and resort to sexual violence (Schlesinger, 1998). It is the entitlement, superiority and vanity domains of narcissism that are most salient in the construct of sexual aggression.

Clearly, however, the low explanatory value of narcissism as a predictor of sexual violence suggests that other variables are at work. Discerning among the multitude of situational, social and personality variables that might explain a greater proportion of variance is a monumental task. It is unlikely that a single, or even a handful of belief structures will overwhelmingly account for a particular criminal act.

Baumeister (2001) reported that narcissists who perceived an insult from a particular other were more likely to be aggressive toward the threatening party, in the narcissistic rages originally identified by Kohut (1972, as cited in Schlesinger, 1998) in reaction to threats against the self-concept. The notion that narcissistic rage reaction against perceived insult can lead to sexual violence was a more specific question than was addressed in this work. However, the results here suggest that future research addressing this particular question could contribute to a more refined understanding about the relationship between narcissism and violence.

Narcissism, Sexual Experience and Sexual Aggression

For the narcissist, it might be difficult to separate sexual experience from sexual aggression. In this work, the participants were only asked to indicate past sexual experience, in comparison with their peers, on a 10-centimeter magnitude estimation response format (*0 –10* anchor points, with *0* indicating minimal or no experience and *10* indicating a great deal of experience). Because the narcissist holds false beliefs about how his victims perceive him and his own actions (Groth, 1979), sexual experience and acts of aggression become entangled. Furthermore, the enhancement-seeking narcissist's braggadocio might lead to exaggeration of past conquests (even on an anonymous survey). It is possible (perhaps likely) that a self-aggrandizing narcissist might over-report what he considers as sexual experience and under-report items involving forced or coerced sex.

This is an especially salient concern when one recalls the nature of the narcissistic power rapist, as discussed in Chapter 4. This type of sexual aggressor deludes himself about the victim's desire for the offender, believing that the victim wants to be raped. These rapists tend to give commands, ask for sexual evaluations from the victim during the rape and try to end the assault as one would complete a date. These offenders often give the victims good-bye kisses, ask for another "date," and drive the victims around after the assault, in a sort of victory lap. A high narcissist power rapist would therefore be unlikely to self-report sexual aggression, as he would not consider his actions to be aggressive. This type of offender might not recognize the wording on the Koss questionnaire of "when she didn't want to" as pertaining to his own actions. Groth (1979) detailed this personality dimension of the power rapist, asserting that these offenders often held the belief that their victims secretly desired the sexual assault.

It should be noted that these extreme examples of highly aggressive rapists were not representative of the sample in this study, but they do illustrate potential directions of behavior for the belief structures investigated here.

Machiavellianism and Sexual Aggression

The second research question dealt with whether Machiavellianism is associated with sexual aggression. Machiavellianism demonstrated a relationship with the dependent variable but is insufficient to explain a significant amount of the variance associated with sexually coercive behavior. Recall that the t–tests indicated a significant relationship between Machiavellianism and sexual aggression but that the coefficient of determination was miniscule.

Machiavellianism was explored as an independent variable in this study to investigate how manipulation, deceit, callousness and cynical self-interest affected the sexually coercive behavior of young men. While this personality construct has been researched in a variety of contexts, its association with sexual aggression has traditionally been neglected in the literature. In investigating this variable's association with sexual aggression, the relationship might be described as positive but modest.

In an attempt to further examine this relationship, one might expect that high Machs would tend be more verbal and manipulative (to include the use of intoxicants) in their sexual coercion, and less likely to use physical force than low Machs. This expectation would be consistent with Grams and Rogers' (1990) assertion that high Machs prefer to use deceit, emotional appeal and other non-direct, manipulative tactics in exerting interpersonal influence on others.

This possibility was examined. Of the SES/SAS items that include some degree of physical force (items 3, 4, 9, and 10), ten participants identified as high Machs reported positive responses, while low Machs reported no positive responses to physical force questions. However, because so few respondents reported using physical force overall ($n = 18$, or 5.84% of the total sample), it is difficult to interpret any meaning from these results. Therefore, the findings of this study do not shed any new light on the question of whether high Machs use more indirect, non-physical tactics to achieve coerced sexual conquest than do other men.

The general aspects of Machiavellianism that are premised to be most instrumental to sexually violent behavior are lack of empathy, a dearth of conventional morality, and manipulative, tactical interactions with others (Christie & Geis, 1970). Furthermore, Boeringer's (1996) research on college athletes and fraternity members suggested that the Machiavellian dynamics of risk-analysis and identification with high-prestige peers (Bogart, Geis, Levy & Zimbardo, 1970) might provide some explanation of the social contexts conducive to sexual aggression. If Machiavellianism was an underlying personality construct of athletes and fraternity members, it might explain a degree of sexually coercive behavior, but only if these participants had significantly higher Mach scores than non-athletes/non-fraternity members.

They did not. Athletic and fraternity participation did not affect the mean Mach scores in this study. The mean Mach scores for athletes and non-athletes were 46.46 and 46.71, respectively. The mean Mach scores for fraternity members and non-fraternity respondents were 46.44 and 46.71, respectively.

Furthermore, sexual aggression scores were not significantly affected by athletic or fraternal membership, as discussed below. Therefore, there was no support in this study for the notion that Machiavellianism acts as an underlying personality construct that encompasses institutionalizes group male activities.

This lack of relationship between Machiavellianism and fraternal or athletic membership relates to the earlier review of the social comparison processes engaged in by high Machs (Bogart et al. 1970). In the prior discussion, it was suggested that if Machiavellians are more apt to engage in dissonant or risky behaviors when they perceive their accomplices to be resourceful and capable (Bogart et al.) then athletic or fraternal Machs might be more sexually aggressive than their counterparts. It was submitted that the socialization and cohesion-building aspects of fraternity membership and/or team athletics might result in the Machiavellian member perceiving his peers as "high prestige partner(s)" (p. 253) and therefore he would be more likely to model deviant activity, in this case sexual aggression.

However, this proposal is not supported in this study. If (as Bogart and his colleagues reported) Machs are more likely to engage in deviant activity when associated with attractive, prestigious comrades, athletic and fraternal affiliation do not provide the triggering social context for this study's sample. It is possible that, regardless of Machiavellian belief structures, men in general do not require formalized groups in order to be sexually aggressive. That is, male peer assemblies might act to support sexually coercive beliefs despite the nature of those groups, be they formalized and institutionalized or not (Schwartz and DeKeseredy, 1997; see also Koss, 1999). This speculation would be consistent with other research that found no significant relationship between fraternity/athletic membership and sexually aggressive tendencies.

The tendency of sexual aggressors to be highly Machiavellian also supports Scully's (1990) characterization of rape as a low-risk endeavor for the aggressor. If sexual aggression is, as Scully proposes, a low-risk activity, the risk-analyzing Mach (Bogart et al., 1970) could be expected to engage in this behavior. Furthermore, Rapaport and Burkhart's (1984) findings that low socialization and responsibility are associated with sexually aggressive behaviors are consistent with the current study's results. These variables are consistent with the Machiavellian aspects of low affect in personal relations, a lack of interest in conventional morality, and low ideological commitment.

However, Rapaport and Burkhart (1984) reported that acceptance of violence was the best predictor of sexual aggression used in their study. It was argued earlier in this work that this could be related to the Machiavellian perception of others as agents of opposition in a hostile world. This was based in part upon Mudrack's (1990) conclusions that the Mach engages in deceit, ingratiation and manipulation in response to an antagonistic society.

However, the current study did not examine attitudes about violence or aggression as an explanatory variable. Therefore, the low proportion of variance in sexual aggression explained by the Mach scores in this study could reflect the absence of violence as a component of Machiavellianism. Some Machs might endorse violence and others might not. Moreover, it is reasonable to believe that the situational context would affect this endorsement, especially given the malleable, tactical outlook of Machs. However, without accounting for individual attitudes towards violence, Machiavellianism remains a construct that is related to sexual aggression but does not explain or predict it.

Athletes and Fraternity Members

As discussed above, athletic and fraternity participation were unrelated to sexual aggression in this sample. These variables were explored in this study as potential social factors in sexual violence. It was hypothesized that the cognitive structures and social comparison processes among individuals who participate in formalized male groups would result in higher reported acts of sexual aggression. This notion was based on past research that demonstrated at least some support for higher sexually aggressive tendencies among these men (Boeringer, 1996; Boeringer, Shehan & Akers, 1991; Crosset & Ptacek, 1996; Ward, Chapman, Cohn, White & Williams, 1991).

However, other research stands in contrast to those findings, deeming these variables as unrelated to sexual aggression (Koss & Gaines, 1993; Schwarz & Nogrady, 1996). Certainly, sampling issues, methodologies, size of institution, alcohol use, and myriad individual and situational variables might account for the difficulty in establishing a clear relationship between athletic and fraternity affiliation and sexual aggression. However, the difficulty in clarifying the relationship might be more a matter of the ubiquitous nature of socialization factors supportive of sexual aggression. Rape-supportive values certainly exist both inside and outside of formalized campus organizations.

In this light, Schwartz and DeKeseredy (1997) proposed a model of male peer support for the emotional and physical abuse of women. This model proposed that the elements of competitive sexual acquisition, social attachment to other men who encourage sexual aggression, narrow conceptions of masculinity, and group values that devalue women combine to form a rape-supportive subculture. These elements are clearly present in at least some fraternities and athletic groups.

However, these authors also make clear that the significance of fraternity membership as a factor in sexual violence often "disappears" in more complex statistical procedures because "what is *really* (emphasis original) causing the problem can be found outside as well as inside fraternities" (Schwartz and DeKeseredy, p. 116). This suggests that social comparisons and the influence of peer groups are not limited to formalized, institutionalized societies. Instead, it seems that one must consider the effects of non-formal peer groups as well as formalized ones in the construction and maintenance of a rape-supportive sub-culture. The form of the group itself might not be a key factor, but the social processes and subcultural values underlying the group could well influence sexually aggressive behavior in formalized and informal peer associations.

In social science terms, of course, this means that one loses a convenient variable to investigate. It is easy to paste on questions about athletic or fraternal membership to a research questionnaire. It is, however, harder to determine what it means when one analyzes the results against variables like sexual aggression. Schwartz and DeKeseredy (1997) rightly point out that underlying social variables are more likely to be responsible for self-reported sexual violence, such as lack of deterrence, group secrecy, and a cohesive sub-culture that condones sexual violence against women. However, these social factors do little to explain the individual cognitive structures of the sexual aggressor. Certainly, they indicate an environment conducive to sexual coercion, if not violence, but they do not touch on the individual mindsets of the perpetrators of rape. It was this individual linkage between social and individual factors of sexual violence that this study attempted to address.

That said, the above-mentioned methodological issues might also account for the mixed findings in past studies of this nature. Koss (1996) identified sampling methodology as one problem in past research that investigated athletic/fraternal participation and sexual violence. For example, Koss pointed out that Schwartz and Nogrady (1996) sampled only three classes, one of which was a class on "sports." Leaving alone the potential problems associated with sampling only three classes, Koss argues that this could have led to an over-sampling of men with an inflated sense of masculinity. Moreover, Schwartz and Nogrady sampled primarily sophomores, juniors and seniors, whereas a previous study by Koss and Gaines (1993) included only freshmen. Koss argues that the increased socialization in formalized peer groups might render older students as better able to exploit others, or conversely, that younger men might hold more stringent belief structures about women that might be later tempered through education and maturation. Either way, Koss stresses the need for cross-sectional, representative samples and the use of longitudinal studies.

Moreover, Koss pointed out the logistical difficulties in attaining useful samples given the sensitive nature of this type of research. Koss maintains that it might be more difficult to attain institutional permission to conduct such research (a problem that did not arise in the current study). To build on Koss's point, it is submitted that there is also a potential difficulty in gaining permission from professors who might, for the best of reasons, be reluctant to allow access to their students for such a sensitive research topic. This reluctance was certainly apparent in this research project.

The sampling plan in the current study included both general education courses and randomly selected colleges. The plan was designed to include students from a wide range of disciplines, as all students were required to take the general education courses that were tapped for this study. Furthermore, the different class levels were well represented, as evidenced by the close proportionate match between the sample and the population for each collegiate grade level (Table 1).

However, it is quite possible that samples drawn from other campuses, perhaps Division I universities might affect the outcome for the athletic variable. For example Crosset and Ptacek (1996) reported that Division I athletes were over-represented in instances of battering and sexual assault as reported to university judicial affairs offices. Benedict (1998) describes a former Division I athlete ("Aaron"- a pseudonym) who was later accused of gang-rape (committed when the individual was a NFL player). Benedict reported: "Along with the instant respect that was afforded Aaron (at college) because of his physical skills, he became the recipient of privileges that fortified his impression that he was not an ordinary college student..." (p. 50).

Perhaps Division I athletes, with the national media attention and prestige attached to their activities and prowess, possess belief systems that are inculcated with feelings of entitlement and impunity from conventional morality. Conversely, it is possible that high-profiled individuals are more likely to attract public scrutiny and stand a greater chance of being accused of criminal activity.

Similarly, institutions of elite wealth and prestige, powered by influential alumnae, might foster fraternities that impart arrogance and risk-taking. Because researchers do not generally name the institutions from which they draw their samples, this potential factor could be difficult to pursue. Furthermore, it would introduce socioeconomic status as yet another variable to be considered.

These speculations transcend mere athletic and fraternity membership, and necessitate the examination of a multitude of other individual and situational variables that cannot be discerned from simple affiliation or non-affiliation with these organizations. Investigation should focus on more fundamental, underlying personality structures of the aggressors as well as the specialized socialization processes acting upon these individuals. An example of this would be Benedict's (1998) work on athletes and rape. Benedict delved into the subculture of athletes in general that fosters rape-supportive attitudes, such as perception of privilege, sexual access, and a low risk for punishment due to their elite status on campus and in greater society.

Athletic and fraternity participation were included in this study not so much to investigate the effect of membership in these groups on sexual aggression per se, but to determine whether the findings would merit further study into cognitive structures that reflect a sexually aggressive belief system, i.e. an entitlement model. Significant findings for these independent variables might have suggested that they could be further studied as two manifestations of entitlement. Entitlement is further discussed below, but as it stands, the current findings offer no support for any hypothesis that would relate these variables to sexual aggression. An entitlement model would have predicted higher aggression among these groups.

Sexual Experience and Sexual Aggression

Self-reported sexual experience had the strongest association with sexual aggression. *T*-tests also revealed a significant difference between high and low sexual experience scores for sexual aggression.

This finding is consistent with the multi-factor model proposed by Malamuth, Heavey and Linz (1993), in which the authors proposed promiscuity as a potential factor of sexual violence among some men. It is perhaps noteworthy that sexual experience also correlated, albeit modestly, with narcissism and Machiavellianism. Both of these correlations were statistically significant at the .01 confidence level. Furthermore, multivariate regression resulted in 9.3% of the variance in sexual experience explained by Machiavellianism and narcissism. This explained proportion exceeds the $\underline{r}^2$ result for sexual aggression scores.

Sexual Acquisitiveness:
This finding suggests that Machiavellianism and narcissism reflect a tendency toward sexual acquisition in general, perhaps as the result of self-servingness and an aggressively persistent approach to women that verges upon and at times crosses the line into coercion. This tendency to target women for sexual access could well result in increased opportunities to aggress against them. It is also possible that the highly Machiavellian or narcissistic male does not recognize or admit to the possibility that he has actually engaged in coercive or assaultive conduct, but was merely engaging in a justified act.

The speculative implication of this finding is that self-gratifying, self-centered, non-empathic belief structures result in higher tendencies for sexually acquisitive behavior. Whether these acquisitive behaviors result in sexually coercive acts or not most likely depends on other individual and situational factors. The SAS/SES scores also depend on the willingness of the participants to self-report past sexual aggression.

These findings concur with Schwartz and DeKeseredy's (1997) statement that research indicates that "acquaintance rapists are hardly those unfortunate men who have trouble attracting women who voluntarily wish to have sex with them" (p. 34). These authors refer to Kanin (1967, as cited in DeKeserdy & Schwartz, 1997) in their argument that "hypererotic" men (p. 34) do not engage in sexual aggression because they are deprived of sex, but because they do not attain as much sex as they believe that they deserve.

Groth (1979) also reported that several rapists informed him that they had girlfriends or wives with whom they could have had sex. These findings indicate that sexual access does not preclude sexual aggression. The premise that men who have high self-regard and feelings of superiority are prone to acquire sex, either through legitimate or illegitimate means, is one that warrants further research.

However, some caution is advised in interpreting the finding that sexual experience is associated with sexual aggression. After all, sexual experience was ultimately found to be an insignificant predictor of sexual aggression in regression tests. Furthermore, this variable was based only on an item in which the participant was requested to indicate his level of sexual experience, compared to his peers, on a 10-centimeter line. While this gives a rough estimate of the individual's self-reported sexual experience, it certainly does not fully explore the variable. The nature of the sexual experience was left open-ended. It could potentially be affected by the narcissism variable (a self-aggrandizing narcissist might tend to exaggerate his experience) and the response was obviously influenced by the participant's perception of peer experience.

Still, it provides some baseline of opportunity to engage in sexual aggression, and offers a rough idea of sexual acquisitiveness. If this variable were to be more fully explored in future research, it would be advisable to decide upon the conceptual nature of sexual experience and operationalize the variable accordingly.

Sexual Experience and Opportunity:
This issue of self-reported experience and opportunity bears further discussion. Does sexual experience, as this study measured it, truly relate to aggression opportunities? It could well depend on how the subject interpreted the item.

A man who has been engaged in a non-aggressive, monogamous sexual relationship for a number of years might consider himself to be as "experienced" as another man who routinely engages in one-time, possibly aggressive relationships with a number of women. The latter individual might frequent bars and parties, assertively and aggressively pursue almost any woman he sees, and essentially go through his life targeting and occasionally achieving new sexual conquests. Clearly, the latter individual has had more opportunity to aggress (and might report higher levels of aggression), but the sexual experience item in this survey does not make these distinctions.

Machiavellianism and Narcissism

This study addressed the question of whether Machiavellianism and narcissism were associated with each other. The results of this study indicate that the two dimensions of personality do share statistically significant correlations in interpersonal manipulation, self-serving tendencies, and lack of empathy for others.

In general, results of this study support McHoskey's (1995) assertion that "both constructs... are associated with similar interpersonal features, e.g., dominance, arrogance and lack of personal warmth" (p. 755). These findings are not surprising, nor were their associations with sexual aggression unexpected.

There is some evidence that narcissists tend to have less stable self-esteem and greater emotional variability than do others (Rhodewalt, Madrian & Cheney, 1998). The narcissists's actions are driven by the need to aggrandize the self and seek attention and admiration. In this way, they could be said to have a cognitive style that continuously seeks self-enhancement. Machiavellians also tend to seek domination or tactical advantage over others in a variety of ways that range from flattery to manipulation to deceit. Machs tend to have a pragmatic and non-idealistic approach to interpersonal situations (Leary, Knight & Barnes, 1986) that suggests a cognitive style that is malleable and situational in nature. However, whether this malleability is linked to an unstable self-esteem is unknown.

Bogart et al. (1970) asserted that high Machs are not so concerned with their self-concepts, and instead make decisions based on gaining tactical advantage in interpersonal exchanges, not in elevating their personal sense of self-worth. However, it was earlier argued in the current study that for the high Mach, gaining a tactical advantage effectively constitutes self-enhancement, and that the Mach's self-worth is tied to winning individual personal exchanges.

It is unknown whether Machiavellians experience the same fluctuations in mood and self-esteem that narcissists do. These issues were not addressed in the current study. However, based on the their tendency to seek advantage over others and to win each interpersonal situation, it could be reasonably argued that Machs are also driven by self-enhancement. The correlations found in this study suggest that some of the beliefs they harbor are similar to those employed by the narcissist: superiority, entitlement, exploitiveness and lack of empathy for others. If narcissists and Machiavellians do demonstrate some shared interpersonal-exchange styles, this could explain the similar correlations in sexual aggression reported in this study.

Feelings of superiority, entitlement, exploitiveness and low empathy appear to be the most salient shared aspects of the two constructs in uncovering a relationship with sexual aggression. However, the fact that neither correlation coefficient is of overwhelming significance necessitates the investigation into other explanatory variables for sexual violence.

Age/Earned Credits and Sexual Aggression

It was surmised that age and collegiate class level would be positively correlated with sexual aggression. There were two points to his premise. First, older students with more general experience and who had longer exposure to campus subculture, would be more socialized with campus peer groups that supported and encouraged the sexual targeting and devaluation of women. Second, the older, more experienced student would have had more opportunities to engage in sexually coercive or violent conduct, simply because of length of time and general experience. However, although age had a mild positive correlation with the dependent variable earned credits did not.

Although the correlation between age and sexual aggression is not sufficient to allow for any definitive interpretations, the results at least suggest that general life experience might have more to do with the propensity to be sexually aggressive than does exposure to campus culture.

The lack of relationship between earned credits and sexual aggression indicates that mere exposure to campus life is not a sufficient factor in predicting sexual aggression. It is possible that many incoming freshmen already hold beliefs about women and sexuality that are hardened and resistant to change. As Schwartz and DeKeseredy (1997) wrote, "...many men come to college with a full armory of ideology and behaviors necessary to abuse women" (p. 144). Therefore, whether these men commit acts of sexual aggression or not could well depend on general experience factors that are unrelated to whether they are college students or not. Because the bulk of this type of research (including the current study) is based on collegiate samples, this could be a noteworthy finding.

Issues of Collegiate Sampling

College students are readily available to the academic investigator. They are convenient for sampling plans and are usually willing to participate in research. Moreover, they possess many of the variables important for this mode of research. They are usually socially active, attend parties (often involving alcohol), and interact with women as friends, dorm-mates, classmates, or as intimates. They tend to be younger and therefore more likely to be sexually acquisitive or aggressive. All of these factors make undergraduate men an attractive group to study for research on sexual aggression.

However, if sexual aggression is more a function of generalized life experience than of college socialization, it behooves researchers to expand their scope into the general community. The insignificance of the fraternity and athletic variables in this study suggest that one need not look only to formalized, university-sanctioned organizations to discover male-oriented peer groups that are rape-supportive, as detailed by Schwartz and DeKeseredy (1997).

Furthermore, it is reasonable to believe that a 21-year-old male with cognitive styles associated with sexual aggression will probably assault women whether he is a college student, a soldier, a factory worker, a supermarket clerk, or a police officer. If age is considered a measure of opportunity and of generalized life experience, then campus life is obviously not the only subculture that presents the occasion to engage in sexual assault.

Research samples drawn from the community at large would transcend campus-related variables and perhaps shed light on sexual violence beyond dorm parties, fraternity mixers, and post-game celebrations. This suggestion is not meant to diminish the importance of campus-culture variables, but to question if and when the personality correlates of sexual aggression hold merit beyond the university walls.

ENTITLEMENT AND SEXUAL AGGRESSION

The Elements of Entitlement

This study proposed the conception of entitlement as a model for sexual violence. This is an introductory model, and the components have only been preliminarily tested in this study. The elements of entitlement are reviewed here:

> The aggrandizement of self, as influenced by cognitive schemas, self-interest, and narrative self-constructions. In his excoriation of the pervasive narcissism embedded in late 20th century culture, Lasch (1979) identified "the theater of everyday life," a phenomenon in which individuals, spurred by a deconstructing culture which questions the existence of an external reality, role play their identities:

To the performing self, the only reality is the identity he can construct out of materials furnished by advertising and mass culture, themes of popular film and fiction, and fragments torn from a vast range of cultural traditions, all of them equally contemporaneous to the contemporary mind (p. 91).

These narrative constructions involve ideation of oneself as a protagonist against a hostile world of others. One manifestation of this is the perception of women as representations of others that are potentially hostile, could inflict injury to the ego, deserve no empathy, and are objects to be used for the protagonist's pleasure.

The protagonist must succeed, and must therefore dominate the hostile others.

The protagonist has a right to do this because of real or perceived wrongs to him (and he therefore deserves revenge), or because he is better than others for some perceived reason (intelligence, physical attractiveness, exceptional ability, wealth).

This study attempted to test the groundwork of the entitlement model by employing established instruments that were consistent with the listed components, that is, the Machiavellianism scale and the Narcissism Personality Inventory. While these scales do not precisely tap the proposed entitlement model, they do measure the central constructs of self-servingness, self-aggrandizement, objectification of others, and superiority that are integral to the entitlement model.

The finding that sexual aggressors tend to be more Machiavellian and narcissistic lends support to the entitlement model. However, the low explanatory coefficients for these variables indicate that the model is deficient in explaining sexual aggression.

One obvious weakness of the model is that it does not include any propensity for violence. Even if an individual held an entitlement belief system, as the model is outlined here, he would not be sexually aggressive if he were not an aggressive person. He might well be a manipulative, self-absorbed, uncaring and unpleasant person, but if he did not endorse or use coercion or violence as a means to achieve his goals, then the model fails.

While cognitive structures that reflect self-interest, superiority and contempt for others seem to be associated with sexual violence, they do not sufficiently explain it (at least in the current study). Some Machiavellian narcissists might merely be annoyed with women who resist their advances and move on to other, more willing partners. Others might use verbal or substance coercion, while still others might carry out violent rapes. Sexual assaults that involve extreme violence, such as sadistic sexual homicides, involve even more psychological variables. There are other belief structures that might be included as well, involving attitudes towards women in general, ideas about toughness and masculinity, or feelings of impunity.

All of this does not preclude the idea of an entitlement model for sexual aggression, only that the model as it stands is incomplete and necessitates further research before it might resemble a useful tool to measure propensity for sexual violence. This model was only introduced here, and was not directly tested. If this model were to be developed, at the least it would include not only the relevant Machiavellian and narcissistic aspects, but would reflect further research into the narrative/protagonist dimensions.

Finally, development of this model would include some element that accounted for a tendency towards violence, as this seemed to be a missing component in explaining sexual aggression in this study. Further discussion on the viability of the entitlement model in conjunction with its cultural narrative component is discussed later in this chapter.

Practical Implications of the Findings

The primary purpose of this study was to add to the theoretical and empirical body of knowledge about sexual aggression. It explored the cognitive structures of Machiavellianism and narcissism and related them to the protagonist/narrative schema model. These constructs were tested for their association with sexual aggression. Sexual experience was investigated to measure opportunity and general sexual acquisitiveness as a variable in sexual aggression. Age and number of credits were measured to determine the socializing effect of general life experience and campus culture.

This model also explored athletic and fraternity participation, for two reasons. One reason was because they had a theoretical linkage with some of the social psychological aspects of narcissism and Machiavellianism, such as social comparison, peer support, and superiority. The other reason was because they had been researched in the past with mixed results, and this study sought to contribute its findings to that body of literature.

Although the main goal of this study was to further the theoretical understanding of sexual aggression, there are some practical implications that are worth discussing. These implications hold relevance primarily for higher education administrators and for those interested in educating both men and women in how to prevent sexual assaults.

The finding that athletic and fraternity participation had no significant effect on sexual aggression suggests that administrators who are concerned only about these organizations should expand their focus. Anti-rape education and sensitivity training should include both men and women, and should be a standard part of freshman orientation programs.

The Message to Women:

Part of this outreach should be directed at women. Women should be educated that they should take precautions not only when attending fraternity/sorority functions, which they might already know, but in any social function. It is unfortunate that one of the implications of this study seems to be that women can never let their guard down. The implication is, rather, that athletes and fraternity members hold no exclusive tendencies for sexual aggression, and that women should not apply a litmus test to men based on their affiliation. Women should habitually take precautions whether they are attending a frat party or a sociology club mixer. These precautions include going out with trusted friends, monitoring alcohol intake, having money for a cab, and in general being aware of their surroundings.

Women should also be educated on the tendencies of sexually aggressive men, as found in this study. While self-absorbed, arrogant, non-empathic, manipulative men with inflated self-concepts are not necessarily sexually aggressive, aggressors do tend to be Machiavellian and narcissistic. Men who interrupt women, who tell misogynist jokes, and who in general demonstrate little respect or empathy for women should be avoided.

This information could be printed on brochures and made available to female students. Faculty, campus police, student life staff, resident advisers, and student organizations could all participate in making these precautionary measures known to female students.

However, the burden of preventing sexual assault should not be placed on women, it should be placed on men. While women should be educated for their own protection, the onus of sexual violence must belong to its primary perpetrators. Delivering a laundry list of forbidden activities to women could be construed as reinforcing the myth that women are responsible for their own victimization.

Standard precautions disseminated to female college students include not accepting drinks from anyone but the bartender, maintaining vigilant watch over their drinks that have been vetted for their consumption, staying in groups with "friends" (peculiar advice perhaps, given the frequency of attacks that were inflicted by male acquaintances and "friends" so perhaps that should be amended to trusting female friends only). Women are further advised to report to dorm- or house-mates where they are going and when they expect to be home, to have their keys out when approaching their cars (ready to be poked through their fists as ready-made weapons in the event of attack), and to stay in well-lit areas with gangs of friends as they navigate across campus in pursuit of their higher education. It seems that women are sometimes advised to live in fear and distrust of almost any social situation, and to lead guarded and barricaded existences.

The intent here is not to degrade the necessity of educating women on how to maintain a relaxed but alert level of awareness, and to make sensible decisions about their actions. Certainly, women should have a healthy cognizance of their surroundings, particularly in social situations involving unknown men, the presence or absence of friends and the availability of intoxicants. All of the above-mentioned precautions are well intentioned, reasonable and important. Women should be made aware of these measures, and educating women could prevent future attacks.

That said, giving women a list of dos and don'ts is insufficient, and ignores the fact that it is men's behavior that should really be changed. Organizations such as Men Against Sexual Violence (MASV) target this point. MASV encourages men to take a stance against sexual assault and promotes the idea that it is up to men to change the ingrained notions that masculinity is somehow equated to sexual aggression.

Attempting to change rape-supportive belief structures of men is more difficult than providing women with a series of commandments that must be followed in order to avoid being victimized. It is also far more crucial. It can only be accomplished through engagement with male peer groups, modeling a protective (as opposed to an aggressive) concept of masculinity, and otherwise undermining beliefs that support the objectification and conquest of women.

Other Practical Implications:
Returning to the direct scope of this study, if sexual violence is perpetrated because the offender believes that it is a low-risk activity (Scully, 1993), which would be consistent with the Machiavellian's risk-analysis behaviors, the findings of this study suggest several policy implications.

Campus police should be empowered to investigate reports of sexual assault, to make arrests, and to forward the offenders for criminal prosecution. They should be trained in how to handle sexual assault complaints, and they should be unencumbered by the administration in doing so. However, campus law enforcement in general has often been obstructed in its duties by administrations that have attempted to suppress reports of rape or sexual assault in order to preserve the institution's image (Boehmer & Parrot, 1993). While university sanctions imposed by collegiate judicial review boards might be appropriate for minor offenses, they should not take the place of criminal proceedings in instances of sexual violence. If Machiavellian sexual aggressors do conduct a risk-analysis in committing sexual aggression, the knowledge that they might be arrested and prosecuted for the crime could serve to deter them.

Regarding the narcissistic element of sexual aggression, the policy implications are not so clear. Treatment strategies that aim at cognitive-behavioral development often focus on empathy development and pointing out the thinking errors of sexual aggressors (Abel & Osborne, 1996). However, these strategies are geared toward the therapeutic treatment of convicted sexual offenders and might not be feasible or appropriate for widespread educational purposes.

The proposition that men come to college already equipped to be abusive towards women suggests the importance of educating males at the high school and even the junior high school level. While parenting classes are often aimed at preventing future parents from abusing their children (Massey, 1998), it is possible that similar classes could also instruct young males on how to be gentle and loving companions to women. Such classes should be taught, if possible, by male faculty and could incorporate peer-relationships into the curriculum. Schwarz and DeKeseredy (1997) suggest the use of student discussion groups that address deeper issues of patriarchy, rape myths, and cultural misogyny. They emphasize the need for integrating university staff from Greek life, athletic personnel, campus police, residential advisors and others to also be trained and sensitized.

Any policy implications should be enacted on the premise that sexual violence is predominantly a male activity. While women should be educated in common-sense precautionary measures, it is really the men who bear the onus for stopping sexual violence.

LIMITATIONS OF THIS STUDY

Sampling and Methodology

Although the current study took extensive measures to construct and implement a careful sampling plan, it is not without its limitations. Because of the population of the university employed in this study, race and ethnicity were not feasible variables. An overwhelming majority of the population is white. Therefore, this study does not address any of the cultural or socioeconomic variables associated with race identified as relevant variables in other studies.

The setting of this study was a mid-sized university in the northeast, and although many students might be from other regions of the U.S., or indeed from other countries, it is primarily a regional institution. The results of this study cannot readily be generalized beyond the population of this particular university. This is perhaps especially so when considering variables such as athletic and fraternity membership, where it is possible that Division I status, wealth and prestige of the university might result in quite different results for the campus "elites."

Moreover, as discussed above, this sample was restricted to undergraduate students. This also limits the usefulness of the findings, in that college samples might vary significantly from community samples in age, racial composition, education, socioeconomic status, and other variables.

While the data collection instruments were inspected and modified to heighten their reliability and validity, the Sexual

Experience item was based on a ten-centimeter line estimation. While the item was carefully worded and provides a good rough baseline of experience, the item is potentially ambiguous, as discussed above.

Another potential limitation of this study is that there were no data collected from women to provide a comparison for the reported prevalence of sexual aggression. The focus of this study was on the attitudes, belief systems and behaviors of men. However, giving the female (victim) version of the Koss SES/SAS to a representative sample of women from the same institution could have provided a validity check about the true prevalence of sexual aggression for this particular sample of respondents. Wide discrepancies between reported rates of victimizing behaviors between the male and female sample might have indicated under-reporting of the behavior from one group or the other. Similar prevalence rates could have suggested that the men in this sample reported honestly. In any event, these data might have been useful.

Inspection of Table 7 discloses that the dependent variable of sexual aggression was unevenly distributed, with a majority (88%) of respondents being non- or low-aggressors and only 12% scoring higher than 2.0 on the SAS/SES. This uneven frequency distribution could represent a possible flaw in the analysis. Because most statistical assumptions include normal distribution of the variables, this could be viewed as another limitation of this study.

Theoretical Limitations

Because the phenomenon of sexual aggression is a multi-factored and complex one, the current study was unable to adequately explain any significant portion of the variance. The most notable omission seems to center on propensity toward violence. While this study identified belief systems (narcissism and Machiavellianism) and behavior (self-reported sexual aggression) that enjoyed high association with sexual aggression, it did not uncover any significant explanation (Proportionate Reduction of Error) for the dependent variable. Because human behavior is complex and multiply determined, this is perhaps to be expected. Still, it is possible that narcissism and Machiavellianism might play a role in predicting sexual violence in future research if items about beliefs in the legitimacy of violence are added.

It is possible that these two cognitive structures were not dissimilar enough to explain sexual aggression. Although they have fundamental differences, they share enough common themes to perhaps miss factors of sexual aggression that might have been picked up by another structural system variable, such as anger control or misogyny. Still, they both demonstrated significant association with sexual aggression, suggesting some relationship, even though it is not an explanatory one.

Criminological research is necessarily limited in seeking to explain or predict criminal behavior. It would be impossible to ascertain all of the personal, social and situational variables that contribute to an individual's commission of an act at a certain time and location against a certain victim. Still, there are broad underpinnings of criminality that may be discerned. It is difficult to tell yet whether the constructs explored here constitute such underpinnings.

CONCLUSIONS

Along with tending toward narcissism and Machiavellianism, the sexual aggressor tends to be sexually acquisitive in general. This suggests that while rape is indeed a crime of violence, there is often a sexual component to the act as well. This lends support to the concept of the "hypererotic" subculture that fosters sexual aggression among certain peer groups (Schwartz & DeKeseredy, 1997), although neither fraternity membership nor athletic participation emerged as significant variables in this study. As suggested by Koss (1999), this could indicate that rape-supportive male peer groups exist outside of institutionalized organizations.

When the sexually acquisitive male targets a woman who is resistant to his advances, Schwartz and DeKeseredy (1997) propose that he might resort to coercion or violence—not out of sexual deprivation, but because the victim is blocking access to a commodity to which he believes he is entitled. The high associations of narcissism and Machiavellianism with sexual aggression found in this study lend support to this proposition. Narcissism drives the angry reaction against the irritating object (the targeted woman), who threatens his self-concept by not giving him the attention and admiration to which he is so richly entitled. Machiavellianism relegates the victim to a hostile other who must be overcome through manipulation, deceit, coercion, or other means, concurrent with the risk involved in committing sexual assault. Both of these constructs are embedded within the aggressor's self-conceptualization as the protagonist in a narrative-style perception of life.

This model would of course work better if there were higher explanatory power among these variables. Although the *t*-tests demonstrate significant association, there are obviously other factors at work that translate these belief structures in to acts of violence. To this end, it might be worthwhile to replicate this study with a dependent variable of rape-supportive attitudes, such as the Acceptance of Rape Myths (ARM) scale as well as the SES/SAS, which focuses only on actual past aggressive acts. Some measure of acceptance of the use of violence would also be useful. These steps might reveal whether many narcissists/Machs reported themselves as non-aggressive because they hold cognitive structures that preclude abusing women, or because they do harbor hostile attitudes toward women but have not acted on them, for whatever reason.

Of course, there is also the real possibility that these respondents did not report their behaviors truthfully on the survey. A personality dimension such as Machiavellianism that is essentially premised on manipulation, deceit and calculated impression management would obviously allow for untruthful responses on a questionnaire, even if anonymity were guaranteed.

As it stands, the current findings are somewhat consistent with the profile of the sexual aggressor as a self-aggrandizing and entitled individual who perceives women as hostile targets. These targets represent interpersonal challenges to the self-concept, and overcoming these obstacles is a challenge that entails manipulation, flattery, guile, deceit, and possibly coercion and violence. Perception of the victim as an object undeserving of empathy, but rather as a hostile other to be acted upon is consistent with both of these constructs. High Machs might conduct a risk-analysis of success before engaging in sexual assault, a risk that unfortunately remains low, given the low reporting rate of victims and the very real possibility that the victim will not be believed by authorities.

THE ROLE OF THE SELF-NARRATIVE

At this point, further discussion of the socially constructed narrative, as a component of the entitlement model, is merited. If the entitlement model were only a collection of personality correlates, it would not be worth even preliminary research or discussion. What makes the entitlement model potentially useful is the dynamic of the cultural narrative structure. Simply testing whether sexual aggressors, or other anti-social individuals, possess some collection of personality characteristics such as deceit or arrogance is not compelling until one can identify the driving mechanism behind the criminal's actions and interactions.

It is here that the Gergen (1988) and Bruner (1990) models of the constructive, meaning-seeking interpretation of reality interact with these personality dimensions in order to produce an assaulter, a rapist, or a killer. These authors formulated the premise that one perceives the self in a particular socially constructed narrative, a story in which the individual is the main character and hero(ine).

According to Bruner, much of this process is culturally-derived, and it is in this context that social variables are significant. Specific social variables are selected by the aggressor to become incorporated into his narrative. Personality dimensions play a role in how someone decides to select and interpret social events and models as they construct their own personal "story." Personality dimensions, whether learned or innate, drive the narrative process and ultimately, the individual's behavior. The narcissist or the Machiavellian assign different values to general external events than say, a highly socially responsible person does. As a result, the narcissist or Mach interprets and selects elements in such way as to construct a meaningful self-narrative in a fundamentally different way than does the socially responsible person. This is so even if the anti-social actor and the pro-social actor are exposed to roughly the same external events.

These "external events" can include routine interactions with a woman at a bar, the police officer, or a university professor. They can also include broader cultural events such as a popular movie, a celebrity murder trial, or a Presidential scandal. All of these will be part of the pool of potential events of meaning that are available to people as they construct and live their personal stories. Their interpretation and use by the individual actor is dependent upon the individual's cognitive style and personality dimensions.

Examples of the Self-Narrative in Action

For example, a sexually abusive man and a compassionate man might both enjoy a police drama in which a rogue cop cuts corners to arrest the bad guys. In this stunningly original formula for a movie, assume the standard components: a divorced, bitter cop who may or may not be avenging the loss a partner, argues with his superiors, ignores laws and procedures in the interests of getting quicker results, may or may not be a martial artist and/or a recovering alcoholic, and is on the trail of fanatically violent serial killer, child murderer, or ritual abuser of some kind.

The sexually abusive man might perceive and assign value to the portrayal of the cop as being a loner and embittered by a divorce (even if the hero is portrayed as not being abusive to women, the underlying bitterness is enough). The assaulter might also like the idea that the cop is defiant to his superiors and breaks the rules in bringing the villain to justice. The cop's masculinity and action-oriented persona is also likely be favorably interpreted by the assaulter. There would no doubt be the theme that the hero is beset on all sides by pencil-necked, nitpicky bureaucrats and foolish, ornamental women who continually get in the way as he does what has to be done. Therefore, the narcissistic, Machiavellian, anti-social man selects and embeds these notions into the self-narrative and perpetuates the corresponding behaviors.

The pro-social man could enjoy the same movie and like the hero as much as the anti-social man does, through different cognitive processes and personality dimensions. While the pro-social man also assigns value to the lonely, embattled cop, his interpretation would be influenced by his essentially responsible tendencies: The hero is driven by a deep, universal morality that transcends the petty departmental regulations; the defiance against his superiors is justifiable because they are either corrupt or incompetent. The cop acts as a protector of women, even though his righteous mission prevents him from becoming involved with them and led to the dissolution of his earlier marriage. His alienation from his superiors and other cops comes from a higher, not a lower, standard of conduct. His aggression and toughness are inflicted only on immensely deserving targets such as sadistic serial killers or child rapists, and his masculinity is tempered by decency. The pro-social man selects these interpreted components and rolls them into a self-narrative that is quite different than the one described above, yet is based on the same external event (the movie).

In this example it is clear that personality dimensions, once formed (at least partly through cognitive structuring) affect how events are interpreted and incorporated into one's personal narrative style, and that this story eventually drives behavior. It is conceded that this model surpasses the data presented in the current study, but that does not preclude theoretical speculation of how the entitlement model may function.

Implications of Entitlement

What needs to be addressed is why the correlative significance emerged for these dimensions, but predictive value remained almost nil, given the many high Machs and narcs and sexually experienced men who were not aggressive.

This finding does not negate the premise described above, it only shows the need to discern the linkage between entitled cognitive styles and physical aggression.

Future research might benefit from determining the most relevant aspects of narcissism, Machiavellianism and sexual acquisition and combining them with attitudes towards the use of violence to achieve one's goals. In this way, perhaps some of the domains of the variables that might not be relevant to sexual violence (such as the leadership or self-sufficiency domains of the NPI) might be stripped out and an instrument that more directly measures sexual entitlement and sexual aggression could be constructed.

It is vital to continue to break down and investigate the psychological structures of the sexually aggressive male. As Schwartz and DeKeseredy (1997) state, "sexual assault will not stop when women take better precautions. It will stop when men stop assaulting women." (pp. 145-146). It is argued here that while women should be educated on how to prevent victimization, it is the belief structures of the assaultive male that should be investigated and countered through education and discussion in order to provide safe environments for women on and off campus.

Entitlement and Other Criminal Acts

Entitlement might serve as a useful model for crimes other than those involving sexual violence. It should be understood that entitlement, or the feeling that one somehow deserves the right to commit a criminal act, is not necessarily restricted to either to people of privilege or status, or to rapists.

A man of low socioeconomic position, who feels frustrated that he does not have the respect from others that he deserves, can also exercise entitlement. Such entitlement could result in vengeance muggings or vandalism against victims whom he perceives to be oppressing him and keeping him from reaching the status that he deserves.

A woman who is a powerful corporate executive may also possess the essential components of entitlement, such as feeling deserving of embezzling from her company, whom she perceives as being run by hostile, yet lowly, fools. Perhaps she has developed entitlement through the constructed "story" that she is a harassed and beleaguered victim who must perform twice as well in the face of continuous gender harassment just to keep her job. In this case, the corporation is a frustrating bully that should be avenged against by the one woman clever and ruthless enough to do it: the protagonist heroine.

The Narrative and the Belief Structures

Note that all of the components of the entitlement model are necessary to facilitate the criminal behavior. Without some type of belief system that approximates the pool of traits represented by Machiavellianism and narcissism, the narrative of victimization and need for vengeance by an embattled heroine (in the above example) might exist as an ideation, but without the dimensions that enable criminal behavior.

Likewise, without the socially constructed narrative, or story, the entitlement dimensions may influence day-to-day interactions, attitudes and behaviors, but they lack the focus, or organizational engine, that translates the floating beliefs and attitudes into the overt criminal act. The narcissist/Machiavellian/entitled individual might be an unpleasant person to be around, but without an impetus of searching for self-meaning (which is how Bruner [1990] describes the psychology of the storied narrative) through criminal activity, this human could be completely lawful, if obnoxious.

Does criminal activity necessitate a self-narrative? This idea may seem absurd if one conceptualizes the socially constructed narrative as a literal, delusional belief in an imaginary existence, one in which the actor actually believes that he or she is some mythical figure of righteous vengeance or destruction. Certainly, psychoses can produce such criminals, but they are quite distinct from the character disorder offenses of interest to this study, and more broadly to the entitled criminal.

To identify self-narrative as a necessary condition for criminal behavior only makes sense if one understands it as Bruner (1990) does. Bruner explains that as persons seek meaning to their lives and their selves, they borrow dramatic symbols of plot from a cultural system and are inculcated into the self. From this premise, one might reasonably presume that actions and behaviors can be derived from these cognitions, and that criminal activity is one such outcome of this model.

SUMMARY

Much of this discussion is of course speculative and theoretical, and goes beyond the scope of the research and data reported in this work. Still, the entitlement model of sexual aggression does have moderate empirical support at this juncture. However, it is conceded that only the barest structures of entitlement have been formulated, and this concept should be considered a work in progress.

An introductory construct, entitlement draws from several established concepts of social and clinical psychology. Entitlement is derived from established personality/character disorders, learning and modeling theory, cognitive scripts and schemas, and social construction literature.

Although this work focused on the problem of sexual aggression, entitlement could potentially emerge as a way of understanding other criminal activity. The cultural symbols that contribute to the criminal self-narrative are universal (the lone defiant hero, vengeance fantasies, the sense of mission, a unique and special individual against the world, the vigorous but embittered protagonist, to name but a few).

Furthermore, the collection of personality characteristics associated with Machiavellianism and narcissism combine to form a rich array of potentially criminal traits that are specifically related to inflated self-regard, arrogance, disregard for moral behavior and a willingness to victimize others for personal gratification. Add to this the free use of rationalization to excuse the behavior, and this concept of entitlement might be contribute to other models of criminal personality (White & Walters, 1989; Yochelson & Samenow, 1976) as a way of understanding the cognitive characteristics of criminal behavior.

It remains to be seen if entitlement can be further developed as an empirically rigorous model of criminality. The viability of any proposed theoretical model, such as the one introduced here, is really. not so crucial. What is of paramount importance is disseminating the idea that the problem of sexual violence transcends the college campus; it transcends gross social or structural variables, and demands the investigation of individual thinking processes of the sexually violent male. Stopping sexual violence against women relies directly upon addressing the beliefs and behaviors of the perpetrators of the aggression. Only then can this problem be properly addressed at the levels of enforcement, prevention, offender and victim treatment, and true understanding of this criminal and social problem.

References

Abel, G. G. & Osborn, C. A. (1996). Behavioral therapy treatment for sex offenders. In I.Rosen (Ed.), *Sexual deviation* (3rd ed). London: Oxford University Press, pp. 382-398.

Allport, G. W. (1958). *The nature of prejudice.* Garden City, NY: Doubleday & Company, Inc.

Allport, G. W. (1937). *Personality: A psychological interpretation.* New York: Henry Holt & Company.

Altabe & Thompson (1996). Body image: A cognitive self-schema construct. *Cognitive Therapy and Treatment, 20* (2), 17). 1-193.

American Psychiatric Association. (1994). *Diagnostic and statistical manual of mental disorders (4th ed.).* Washington, DC: Author.

Apt, C. & Hulbert, D. F. (1995). Sexual narcissism: Addiction or anachronism? *Family Journal, 3* (2), 103-107.

Armentrout, J. A. & Hauer, A. L. (1978). MMPIs of rapists of adults, rapists of children, and nonrapist sex offenders. *Journal of Clinical Psychology, 34,* 330-332.

137

Aronson, E. (1968). Dissonance theory: Progress and problems. In R. Abelson, E. Aronson, W. McGuire, T. Newcomb, M. Rosenberg, & P. Tannenbaum (Eds.), *Theories of cognitive consistency: A sourcebook.* (pp. 5-27). Chicago: Rand McNally.

Babbie, E. (1998). *The practice of social research (8ᵗʰ ed.).* Belmont, CA: Wadworth Press.

Bandura, A. (1977). *Social learning theory.* Englewood Cliffs, NJ: Prentice Hall.

Baumeister, R. (2001). Violent pride: Do people turn violent because of self-hate, or self-love? *Scientific American,* 96-101.

Beall, A. E. (1993). A social constructionist view of gender. In A. E. Beall & R. J. Sternberg (Eds.), *The psychology of gender* (pp. 127-147). New York: Guilford Press.

Bem, D. (1970). *Beliefs, attitudes, and human affairs.* Belmont, CA: Brooks/Cole.

Benedict, J. R. (1998). Athletes and acquaintance rape. Thousand Oaks, CA: Sage Publishing.

Bernat, J. A., Calhoun, K. S. & Stolp, S. (1998). Sexually aggressive men's responses to a date rape analogue: A disinhibiting cue. *The Journal of Sex Research, 35,* 341.

Berkowitz, L. & Devine, P. G. (1995). Has social psychology always been cognitive? What is "cognitive" anyhow? *Personality and Social Psychology Bulletin, 21,* 696-703.

Big Five personality factors. [On-Line]. Available: www.carleton.ca/~tpychyl/01138/BigFive.html

Blalock, H. M. (1979). *Social statistics (Rev. 2ⁿᵈ ed.).* New York: McGraw-Hill.

Blau, P. (1953). Orientation of college students toward international relations. *American Journal of Sociology*, 59, 205-214.

Boeringer, S. B. (1996). Influences of fraternity membership, athletics and male living arrangements on sexual aggression. *Violence Against Women, 2* (2), 134-147.

Boeringer, S. B., Shehan, C. L., & Akers, R. L. (1991). Social contexts and social learning in sexual coercion and aggression: Assessing the contribution of fraternity membership. *Family Relations, 40*, 58-64.

Bogart, K., Geis, F. L., Levy, M., & Zimbardo, P. (1970). No dissonance for Machiavellians. In R. Christie & F. L. Geis (Ed.). *Studies in Machiavellianism* (pp. 53-95). New York: Academic Press.

Boehmer, C. & Parrot, A. (1993). *Sexual assault on campus*, New York: Lexington Books.

Borgatta, E. F. (1964). The structure of personality characteristics. *Behavioral Science, 9*, 8-17.

Brewer, M. B. (1988). A dual process model of impression formation. In T. K. Srull (Ed.), *Advances in social cognition, volume one* (pp. 1-36). Hillsdale, NJ: Lawrence Earlbaum Associates, Inc.

Brownmiller, S. (1975). *Against our will: Men, women and rape.* New York: Simon and Schuster.

Bruner, J. (1990). *Acts of meaning.* Cambridge, MA: Harvard University Press.

Burgess, A.W. & Holmstrom, L. L. (1985). Rape trauma syndrome and Post Traumatic Stress Disorder. In A. W. Burgess (Ed.) *Rape and sexual assault: A research handbook* (pp. 46-60). New York: Garland Publishing, Inc.

Burt, M. (1980). Cultural myths and supports for rape. *Journal of Personality and Social Psychology, 38,* 217-230.

Calhoun, K. S., Atkeson, B. M., & Resick, P. A. (1982). A longitudinal examination of fear reactions in victims of rape. *Journal of Counseling Psychology, 29* (6), 655-661.

Calhoun, K. S. & Bernat, J. A. (1997). Sexual coercion and attraction to sexual aggression in a community sample of young men. *Journal of Interpersonal Violence, 12,* 392-406.

Cantor, N. & Kihlstrom, J. F. (1990). Social intelligence and cognitive assessments. In R. S. Wyer, Jr. & T. K. Srull (Eds.), *Advances in social cognition Vol. 2,* pp. 1-59.

Cattell, R. B. (1933). Temperament tests. II: Tests. *British Journal of Psychology,* 23, 308-329.

Christensen, L. B. & Stoup, C.M. (1986). *Introduction to statistics for the social and behavioral sciences (2nd ed.).* Pacific Grove, CA: Brooks/Cole Publishing.

Christie, R., & Geis, F. L. (1970). *Studies in Machiavellianism.* New York: Academic Press.

Corral, S. & Calvete, E. (1999). Machiavellianism: Dimensionality of the Mach IV and its relation to self-monitoring in a Spanish sample. *Spanish Journal of Psychology, 3* (1), 3-13.

Costa, P.T., Jr. & McCrae, R. R. (1985). *The NEO Personality Inventory Manual.* Odessa, FL: Psychological Assessment Resources.

Crosset, T. W., Ptacek, J., McDonald, M. A., & Benedict, J. R. (1996). Male student-athletes and violence against women: A survey of campus judicial affairs offices. *Violence Against Women, 2,* 163-179.

Dean, K. E. & Malamuth, N. M. (1997). Characteristics of men who aggress sexually and of men who imagine aggressing. *Journal of Personality and Social Psychology, 72* (2), 449-455.

Deaux, K. & Wrightsman, L. S. (1984). *Social psychology in the 80s.* Pacific Grove, CA: Brooks/Cole Publishing.

DeVellis, R. F. (1991). *Scale development: Theory and applications.* Thousand Oaks, CA: Sage Publishing.

Devine, P.G., Monteith, M.J., Zuwerink, J. R. & Eliot, A.J. (1991). Prejudice with and without compunction. *Journal of Personality and Social Psychology, 60* (6), 817-830.

Digman, J. M. (1997). Higher-order factors of the Big Five. *Journal of Personality and Social Psychology, 73,* 1246-1256.

Digman, J. M. & Inouye, J. (1986). Further specification of the five robust factors of personality. *Journal of Personality and Social Psychology, 50,* 116-123

Digman, J. M. & Takemoto-Chock, (1981). Factors in the natural language of personality: Re-analysis and comparison of six major studies. *Multivariate Behavioral Research, 16,* 475-481.

Driscoll, J. M., Allais-Hulin, V. & Bagg-Mayer, V. (1997). Feelings of mastery in aggressors: A conceptual replication of an American experiment in France. *Journal of Social Psychology, 137,* 777-781.

Drout, C., Becker, T., Bukkosy, S., & Mansell, M. (1994). Does social influence mitigate or exacerbate responsibility for rape? *Journal of Social Behavior and Personality, 9,* 409-420.

Dunn, P.C., Vail-Smith, K. & Knight, S. M. (1999). What date/acquaintance rape victims tell others: A study of college student recipients of disclosure. *Journal of American College Health, 47* (5), 213-219.

Eliot, A. J. & Devine, P. G. (1994). On the motivational nature of cognitive dissonance: Dissonance as psychological discomfort. *Journal of Personality and Social Psychology, 67* (3), 382-394.

Ellis, L. (1989). *Theories of rape.* New York: Hemisphere Publishing Company.

Emmons, R. A. (1987). Narcissism: Theory and measurement. *Journal of Personality and Social Psychology, 52* (1), 11-17.

Exline, R. V., Thibault, J., Hickey, C. B., & Gumpert, P. (1970). Visual interaction in relation to Machiavellianism and an unethical act. In R. Christie & F. L. Geis (Ed.), *Studies in Machiavellianism* (pp. 53-95). New York: Academic Press.

Federal Bureau of Investigation, Uniform Crime Report (2000). [On-line]. Available: www.fbi.gov

Festinger, L. (1954). A theory of social comparison processes. *Human Relations, 7*, 117-140.

Festinger, L. (1957). *A theory of cognitive dissonance.* Stanford, California: Stanford University Press.

Finn, P. (1995). *Preventing alcohol-related problems on campus: Acquaintance rape. Higher Education Center for Alcohol and Other Drug Prevention,* U.S. Department of Education (ED/ORE95-7). Washington, DC: U.S. Department of Education.

Fiske, D. W. (1949). Consistency of factorial structures of personality ratings from different sources. *Journal of Abnormal Social Psychology, 44,* 329-344.

Frank, E., Anderson, B., Stewart, B. D., Dancu, C., West, D. (1988). Efficacy of cognitive behavior therapy and systematic desensitization in the treatment of rape trauma. *Behavior Therapy, 19,* 403-420.

Gable & Dangello (1994). Locus of control, Machiavellianism and managerial job performance. *The Journal of Psychology, 128* (5), 599-608.

Gergen, K. J. (1994). *Realities and relationships: Soundings in social construction.* Cambridge, MS: Harvard University Press.

Gergen, K. J. & Gergen, M. M. (1988). Narrative and the self as relationship. In L. Berkowitz (Ed.), *Advances in experimental social psychology, Vol. 21. Social psychological studies of the self: Perspectives and paradigms.* (pp. 17-56). San Diego: Academic Press, Inc.

Gilbert, N. (1998). Realities and mythologies of rape. *Society, 35* (2), 356-361.

Gilligan, J. (1996). *Violence: Reflections on a national epidemic.* New York: Random House.

Goldberg, L. R. (1981). Language and individual differences: The search for universals in personality lexicons. In L. Wheeler (Ed.), *Personality and social psychology review, Vol. 2* (pp. 141-165). Beverly Hills, CA: Sage.

Gough (1957). *California Psychological Inventory.* Palo Alto, CA: Consulting Psychologists Press.

Grams, W. C. & Rogers, R. W. (1990). Power and personality: Effects of Machiavellianism, need for approval and motivation on influence tactics. *Journal of General Psychology, 117* (1), 71-93.

Greenwald, A. G. (1980). The totalitarian ego: Fabrication and revision of personal history. *American Psychologist, 35* (7), 603-618.

Greenwald, A. G., & Banaji, M. R. (1995). Implicit social cognition: Attitudes, self-esteem, and stereotypes. *Psychological Review, 102,* 4-27.

Groth, N. (1979). *Men who rape: The psychology of the offender.* New York: Plenum Press.

Haines, S. C., Hogg, M. A. & Duck, J. M. (1997). Self-categorization and leadership: Effect of group prototypicality and leader stereotypicality. *Personality and Social Psychology Bulletin, 23,* 1087-1099.

Hersh, K. & Gray-Little, B. (1998). Psychopathic traits and attitudes associated with self-reported sexual aggression in college men. *Journal of Interpersonal Violence, 13,* 456-471.

Indiana University of Pennsylvania, Crime Statistics (2000). [On-line].
    Available: www.iup.edu/studentaffairs/safety/indiana.shtm

Irwin, H. J. (1995). Codependence, narcissism, and childhood trauma. *Journal
    of Clinical Psychology, 51* (5), 658-665.

Janoff-Bulman, R., Timko, C., & Carli, L. L. (1985). Cognitive biases in
    blaming the victim. *Journal of Experimental Social Psychology, 21,* 161-
    177.

John, O. P., Angleitner, A. & Ostendorf, F. (1988). The lexical approach to
    personality: A historical review of trait taxonomic research. *European
    Journal of Personality, 2,* 171-205.

Joubert, C. E. (1998). Narcissism, need for power, and social interest.
    Psychological Reports, 82, 701-702.

Kalof, L. (1993). Dilemmas of femininity: Gender and the social construction
    of sexual imagery. *Sociological Quarterly, 34,* 639-651.

Kellogg, R. (1995). *Cognitive psychology.* Thousand Oaks, CA: Sage
    Publishing.

Kelly, G. (1963). *A theory of personality: The psychology of personal
    constructs.* New York: W.W. Norton & Company.

Kerr, A. E., Patton, M.J., Lapan, R.T. & Hills, H. (1994). Interpersonal
    correlates of narcissism in adolescents. *Journal of Counseling and
    Development (73),* 2, 204-210.

Knight, M. (1994). Darwinian functionalism: A cognitive science paradigm.
    Psychological Record, 44, 271-287.

Kopelman, R. E. & Mullins, L. S. (1992). Is narcissism inversely related to
    satisfaction? An examination of data from two U.S. samples. *Journal of
    Psychology, 126* (2), 121-130.

Kohut, H. (1972). Thoughts on narcissism and narcissistic rage. *Psychoanalytic Study of the child, 27,* 360-400.

Koss, M. P., & Cleveland, H. H. (1997). Stepping on toes: Social roots of date rape lead to intractability and politicization. In M. D. Schwartz (Ed.), *Researching sexual violence against women: Methodological and personal perspectives* (pp. 4-21). Thousand Oaks, CA: Sage Publications.

Koss, M. P. & Cleveland, H. H. (1996). Athletic participation, fraternity membership, and date rape: The question remains—self-selection or different causal process? *Violence Against Women, 2* (2), 180-190.

Koss, M. P., & Gaines, J. A. (1993). The prediction of sexual aggression by alcohol use, athletic participation, and fraternity affiliation. *Journal of Interpersonal Violence, 8* (1), 94-108.

Koss, M.P. & Gidycz, C.A. (1985). Sexual experiences survey: Reliability and validity. *Journal of Consulting and Clinical Psychology,* 53, 422-423.

Koss, M.P., Gidycz, C.A., & Wisniewski, N. (1987). The scope of rape: Incidence and prevalence of sexual aggression and victimization in a national sample of higher education students. *Journal of Consulting and Clinical Psychology,* 55, 162-170.

Koss, M.P, & Oros, C. (1982). Sexual experiences survey: A research instrument investigating sexual aggression and victimization. *Journal of Consulting and Clinical Psychology, 50,* 455-457.

Kosson, D. S. & Kelly, J. C. (1997). Psychopathy-related traits predict self-reported sexual aggression among college men. *Journal of Interpersonal Violence, 12,* 241-254.

Lambourn, B. & Day, H. D. (1995). Characteristics of male partners of adult female incest survivors. *Journal of Contemporary Psychotherapy, 25* (4), 387-398.

Lanier, C. A., Elliott, M. N., Martin, D. W., Kapadia, A. (1998). Evaluations of an intervention to change attitudes toward date rape. *College Teaching, 46* (2), 76-78.

Lansky, M. R. (1995). Nightmares of a hospitalized rape victim. *Bulletin of the Menninger Clinic, 59*, 4-14.

Lasch, C. (1979). *The culture of narcissism.* New York: W. W. Norton & Company, Inc.

Lewin, K. (1997). *Resolving social conflicts and field theory in social science.* Washington, DC: American Psychological Association.

Lewis-Beck, M. (1980). *Applied regression: An introduction.* Thousand Oaks, CA: Sage Publishing.

Lipset, S. M., Lazarsfeld, P., Barton, A. & Linz, J. (1954). The psychology of voting: An analysis of political behavior. In G. Lindzey (Ed.), *Handbook of social psychology,* Vol. II. Cambridge, MA: Addison-Wesley.

Lisak, D. & Ivan, C. (1995). Deficits in intimacy and empathy in sexually aggressive men. *Journal of Interpersonal Violence, 10* (3), 296-308.

Machiavelli, N. (1940). *The discourses.* New York: Modern Library.

Machiavelli, N. (1966). *The prince.* New York: Bantam.

Malamuth, N. M. (1981).Rape proclivities among males. *Journal of Social Issues, 29*, 138-157.

Malamuth, N. M. (1983). Factors associated with rape as predictors of laboratory aggression against women. *Journal of Personality and Social Psychology, 45*, 432-442.

Malamuth, N. M. (1986). Predictors of naturalistic sexual aggression. *Journal of Personality and Social Psychology, 50*, 953-962.

Malamuth, N. M. (1989). The attraction to sexual aggression scale: Part one. *The Journal of Sex Research, 26*, (1), 26-49.

Malamuth, N. M., & Check, J. V. P. (1985). The effects of aggressive pornography on beliefs in rape myths: Individual differences. *Journal of Research in Personality, 19*, 299-320.

Malamuth, N. M., Feshbach, S., & Jaffem Y. (1977). Sexual arousal and aggression: Recent experiments and theoretical issues. *Journal of Social Issues, 33* (2), 110-133.

Malamuth, N. M., Heavey, C. L., & Linz, D. (1993). Predicting men's antisocial behavior against women: The interaction model of sexual aggression. In G. C. N. Hall, R. Hirschman, J. R. Graham, & M. S. Zaragoza (Eds.), *Sexual aggression: Issues in etiology, assessment, and treatment* (pp. 63-91). Washington, D.C.: Taylor & Francis.

Malamuth, N.M., Sockloskie, R.J., Koss, M.P. and Tanaka, J.S. (1991). Characteristics of aggressors against women: Testing a model using a national sample of college students. *Journal of Consulting and Clinical Psychology, 59* (5), 670-681.

Mandler, G. (1984). Origins and range of contemporary cognitive psychology. *Zeitshcrift fuer Psychologie, 192* (1), 73-85.

Markus, H. (1977). Self-schemata and processing information about the self. *Journal of Personality and Social Psychology, 35*, 63-78.

Markus, H. & Nurius, P. (1986). Possible selves. *American Psychologist, 41* (9), 954-969.

Martin, R. (1985). Perception of self and significant others in assaultive and non-assaultive criminals. *Journal of Police and Criminal Psychology (2)*, 2-13.

Massey, M. S. (1998). *Early childhood violence prevention.* (Report No. EDO-PS-98-9). Washington, D.C.: Office of Educational Research and Improvement (ED). (ERIC Document Reproduction Service No. ED424032).

Masterson, J. F. (1981). *The narcissistic and borderline disorders: An integrated developmental approach.* New York: Brunner/Mazel Publishers.

Maxwell, M.G. & Babbie, E. (2000). *Research methods for criminal justice and criminology.* Belmont, CA: Wadsworth/Thomson.

Mayer, R. A. & Ottens, A. J. (1994). Holistic treatment of rape victims. *Guidance and Counseling, 9,* 421-428.

McAdams, D. P. (1992). The five-factor model in personality: A critical appraisal. *Journal of Personality, 60* (2), 329-361.

McCrae, R. R. & Costa, P. T. (1989). More reasons to adapt the five-factor model. *American Psychologist, 44,* 451-452.

McCaw, J. M. & Senn, C. Y. (1998). Perception of cues in conflictual dating situations. *Violence Against Women, 98,* 609-624.

McHoskey, J. W. (1999). Machiavellianism, intrinsic versus extrinsic goals, and social interest: A self-determination theory analysis. *Motivation and Emotion, 23* (4), 267-283.

McHoskey, J. W. (1995). Narcissism and Machiavellianism. *Psychological Reports, 77,* 755-759.

McLendon, K., Foley, L. A., Hall, J., Sloan, Lauriann, Wesley, A., & Perry, L. (1994). Male and female perceptions of date rape. *Journal of Social Behavior and Personality, 9,* 421-428.

Medin, D. L. (1988). Social categorization: Structures, processes, and purposes. In T. K. Srull & R. S. Wyer, Jr. (Eds.), *Advances in social cognition: A dual process model of impression formation* (pp. 119-126).

Messerschmidt, J. W. (1993). *Masculinities and crime: Critique and reconceptualization of theory.* Lanham, MD: Rowman & Littlefield Publishers, Inc.

Meyer, S., Vivian, D. & O'Leary, K. D. (1998). Men's sexual aggression in marriage. *Violence Against Women, 4* (4), 415-435.

Miller (1997). *Egotopia*. Tuscaloosa, AL: University of Alabama Press.

Mischel, W. (1973). Toward a cognitive social learning reconceptualization of personality. *Psychological Review, 30* (4), 252-283.

Moore, S. R., Ward, M., & Katz, B. (1998). Machiavellianism and tolerance of ambiguity. *Psychological Reports, 82* (2), 415-418.

Moore, S. R., Smith, R. E. & Gonzalez, R. (1997). Personality and judgement heuristics: Contextual and individual difference interactions in social judgment. *Personality and Social Psychology Bulletin, 23,* 76-83.

Mudrack, P. E. (1990). Machiavellianism and locus of control: A meta-analytic review. *The Journal of Social Psychology, 130* (1), 125-126.

Mullins, L. S. & Kopelman, R. E. (1988). Toward an assessment of the construct validity of four measures of narcissism. *Journal of Personality Assessment, 52* (4), 610-625.

Norman, W. T. (1963). Toward an adequate taxonomy of personality attributes: Replicated factor structure in peer nomination personality rating. *Journal of Abnormal and Social Psychology, 66* (6), 574-583.

Nunnally, J. C. (1978). *Psychometric theory (2nd ed.)*. New York: McGraw-Hill.

Nurius, P. S. & Norris, J. (1996). Expectations regarding acquaintance sexual aggression among sorority and fraternity members. *Sex Roles, 35,* (7/8), 427-444.

Pakaslahti, L. & Keltikangas-Jarvinen, L. (1997). The relationships between moral approval of aggression, aggressive problem-solving strategies, and aggressive behavior in 14-year-old adolescents. *Journal of Social Behavior and Personality, 12,* 905-924.

Piaget, J. (1948). *The moral judgment of the child.* New York: Free Press.

Poole, P. P. & Gray, B. (1990). Organizational script development through interactive accommodation. *Group and Organization Management, 15,* 212-232.

Rada, R. T. (1978). *Clinical aspects of the rapist.* New York: Grune & Stratton.

Rader, C. M. (1977). MMPI profile types of exposers, rapists, and assaulters in a court services population. *Journal of Consulting and Clinical Psychology, 45* (1), 61-69.

Rando, R. A., Rogers, J. R. & Britan-Powell, C. S. (1998). Gender role conflict and college men's sexually aggressive attitudes and behavior. *Journal of Mental Health Counseling, 20,* 359-369.

Rapaport, K. & Burkhart, B. (1984). Personality and attitudinal characteristics of sexually coercive college males. *Journal of Abnormal Psychology, 93,* 216-221.

Raskin, R. R. & Hall, C. S. (1979). Narcissistic Personality Inventory. *Psychological Reports, 45,* 450.

Rescher, N. (1979). *Cognitive systematization.* Totowa, NJ: Rowman and Littlefield.

Resick, P. A., Veronen, L. J., Kilpatrick, D. G., Calhoun, K. S. & Atkeson (1986). Assessment of fear reactions in sexual assault victims: A factor analytic model of the Veronen-Kilpatrick Modified Fear Survey. *Behavioral Assessment, 8* (3), 271-283.

Ressler, R. K., Burgess, A. W., & Douglas, J. E. (1988). *Sexual homicide: Patterns and motives.* Lexington, Massachusetts: D.C. Heath and Company.

Rhodewalt, F., Madrian, J. C. & Cheney, S. (1998). Narcissism, self-knowledge organization, and emotional reactivity: The effect of daily experiences on self-esteem and affect. *Personality and Social Psychology Bulletin, 24,* 75-87.

Rubenzahl, S. A. (1998). The prevalence and characteristics of male perpetrators of acquaintance rape: New methodology reveals new findings. *Violence Against Women, 4,* 713-725.

Sadowski, C. J. & Cogburn, H. E. (1997). Need for cognition in the Big-Five factor structure. *Journal of Psychology, 131,* 307-312.

Salmivalli, C. & Kaukiainen, A. (1999). Self-evaluated self-esteem, peer-evaluated self-esteem, and defensive egotism as predictors of adolescents' participation in bullying situations. *Personality and Social Psychology Bulletin, 25,* 1268-1278.

Schlesinger, L. B. (1998). Pathological narcissism and serial homicide: Review and case study. *Current Psychology, 17* (2/3), 212-220.

Scholl, R.W. (1999). *Social Cognition and Cognitive Schemas* [On-line]. Available: www.cba.uri.edu/Scholl/Notes/Cognitive_Schema.htm

Schulte, H. M. & Hall, M. J. (1994). Violence in patients with narcissistic personality pathology: Observations of a clinical series. *American Journal of Psychotherapy, 48* (4), 610-623.

Schwartz, M. D. (1999). *Researching sexual violence against women: Methodological and personal perspectives.* Thousand Oaks, CA: Sage Publishing.

Schwartz, M. D. & DeKeseredy, W.S. (1997). *Sexual assault on campus: The role of male peer support.* Thousand Oaks, CA: Sage Publishing.

Schwartz, M. D. & Nogrady, C.W. (1996). Fraternity membership, rape myths, and sexual aggression on a college campus. *Violence Against Women,* 2 (2), 148-162.

Scott, C.F., Madura, M. & Weaver, L. (1998). Premarital sexual aggressors: multivariate analysis of social, relational and individual variables. *Journal of Marriage and the Family, 60* (1), 56-69.

Scully, D. (1990). *Understanding sexual violence: A study of convicted rapists.* New York: Harper Collins Academic.

Shively, M. & Lam, J. A. (1991). Sampling methods and admissions of sexual aggression among college men. *Deviant Behavior: An Interdisciplinary Journal, 12,* 345-360.

Shulman, D. G. & Ferguson, G. R. (1988). Two methods of assessing narcissism: Comparison of the Narcissism-Projective (N-P) and the Narcissistic Personality Inventory (NPI). *Journal of Clinical Psychology, 44,* 857-866.

Sims, H. P. & Lorenzi, P. (1992). *The new leadership paradigm: Social learning and cognition in organizations.* Thousand Oaks, CA: Sage Publications, Inc.

Skinner, N. (1989). Personality correlates of Machiavellianism: VI. Machiavellianism and the psychopath. *Social Behavior and Personality, 16* (1), 33-37.

Spaccarelli, S. & Bowden, B. (1997). Psychosocial correlates of male sexual aggression in a chronic delinquent sample. *Criminal Justice and Behavior, 24,* 71-95.

Struckman-Johnson, C. (1997). From acquaintance rapists to incarcerated sexual offenders: A categorical model for male sexual aggression. *Journal of Sex Research, 34,* 319-321.

Sugarman, D. B. (1994). The conception of rape: A multidimensional scaling approach. *Journal of Social Behavior and Personality, 9,* 389-408.

Sugarman, D. B. & Hotaling, G. T. (1989). Violent men in intimate relationships: An analysis of risk markers. *Journal of Applied Social Psychology, 19,* 1034-1048.

Sullivan, E. H. (1947). *Principles of criminology (4th ed.)*. Philadelphia: J.B. Lippincott.

Svrakic, D. (1990). The functional dynamics of the narcissistic personality. *American Journal of Psychotherapy, 44* (2), 189-203.

The big 5 factors and illustrative adjectives. [On-line]. Available: fmarion.edu/~personality/corr/big5/traits.html.

Truman, D. M. & Tokar, D. M. (1996). Dimensions of masculinity: Relations to date rape supportive attitudes and sexual aggression in dating situations. *Journal of Counseling and Development, 74* (6), 555-562

Tupes, E. C. & Christal, R. E. (1961). Recurrent personality factors based on trait ratings. USAF Aeronautical Systems Division Technical Report. No. 61-97.

Tupes, E. C. & Kaplan, M. N. (1961). Relationship between personality traits, physical proficiency, and cadet effectiveness reports of Air Force Academy cadets. USAF Aeronautical Systems Division Technical Note. No. 61-53.

Vander Zanden. (1984) *Social psychology (3rd ed.)*. New York: Random House.

Ward, S. K., Chapman, K., White, S. & Williams, K. (1991). Acquaintance rape and the college social scene. *Family Relations, 40* (1), 65-71.

Watson, P. J. & Biderman, M. D. (1993). Narcissistic Personality Inventory factors, splitting and self-consciousness. *Journal of Personality Assessment, 61* (1), 41-57.

Watson, Biderman & Sawrie (1994). Empathy, sex role orientation, and narcissism. *Sex Roles: A Journal of Research, 30,* 701-723.

Watson, P. J. & Hickman, S. E. (1995). Narcissism, self-esteem and parental nurturance. *Journal of Psychology, 129* (1), 61-73.

Weisburd, D. (1998). *Statistics in Criminal Justice.* Stamford, CT: Wadsworth.

Weisz, M. G., & Earls, C. M. (1995). The effects of exposure to filmed sexual violence on attitudes toward rape. *Journal of Interpersonal Violence, 10,* 71-83.

White, C. (1993). Relationships between assertiveness, Machiavellianism, and interviewing success in a screening interview. *Psychological Reports, 73,* 1209-1210.

White, T.W. & Walters. G.D. (1989). Lifestyle criminality and the psychology of disresponsibility. *International Journal of OffenderTherapy and Comparative Criminology, 33* (3), 257-263.

Wood, J. V. (1989). Theory and research concerning social comparisons of personal attributes. *Psychological Bulletin, 106,* 231-248.

Yescavage, K. (1999). Teaching women a lesson: Sexually aggressive and sexually nonaggressive men's perceptions of acquaintance and date rape. *Violence Against Women, 5,* 796-812.

Yochelson, S. & Samenow, S.E. (1976). *The criminal personality.* Northvale, NJ: Aronson.

Young, J. E. & Lindemann, M. D. (1992). An integrative schema-focused model for personality disorders. *Journal of Cognitive Psychotherapy, 6* (1), 11-23.

Appendix A:
Sexual Experiences Survey (Koss, Gidycz & Wisniewski, 1987). Modified to Likert format for increased sensitivity of measure.

1. Have you ever had a woman give in to sex play (fondling, kissing, or petting, but not intercourse) when she didn't want to because you overwhelmed her with continual arguments and pressure?

_____ Never
_____ Rarely
_____ Sometimes
_____ Often
_____ Very often

2. Have you had sex play (fondling, kissing, or petting, but not intercourse) with a woman who didn't want to because you used your position of authority (boss, teacher, camp counselor, supervisor) to make her?

_____ Never
_____ Rarely
_____ Sometimes
_____ Often
_____ Very often

3. Have you had sex play (fondling, kissing, or petting, but not intercourse) with a woman who didn't want to because you threatened or used some degree of physical force (twisting her arm, holding her down, etc.) to make her?

____ Never
____ Rarely
____ Sometimes
____ Often
____ Very often

4. Have you attempted sexual intercourse with a woman (getting on top of her, attempting to insert your penis) when she didn't want to by threatening or using some degree of force (twisting her arm, holding her down, etc.) but intercourse did *not* occur?

____ Never
____ Rarely
____ Sometimes
____ Often
____ Very often

5. Have you attempted sexual intercourse with a woman (getting on top of her, attempting to insert your penis) when she didn't want to by giving her alcohol or drugs, but intercourse did *not* occur?

____ Never
____ Rarely
____ Sometimes
____ Often
____ Very often

6. Have you had sexual intercourse with a woman when she didn't want to because you overwhelmed her with continual arguments and pressure?

____ Never
____ Rarely
____ Sometimes
____ Often
____ Very often

7. Have you had sexual intercourse with a woman who didn't want to because you used your position of authority (boss, teacher, camp counselor, supervisor) to make her?

____ Never
____ Rarely
____ Sometimes
____ Often
____ Very often

8. Have you had sexual intercourse with a woman who didn't want to because you gave her alcohol or drugs?

____ Never
____ Rarely
____ Sometimes
____ Often
____ Very often

9. Have you had sexual intercourse with a woman when she didn't want to by threatening or using some degree of force (twisting her arm, holding her down, etc.) to make her?

____ Never
____ Rarely
____ Sometimes
____ Often
____ Very often

10. Have you had sex acts (anal or oral intercourse or penetration by objects other than the penis) with a woman who didn't want to because you threatened or used some degree of physical force (twisting her arm, holding her down, etc.) to make her?

_____ Never
_____ Rarely
_____ Sometimes
_____ Often
_____ Very often

Appendix B:
Social Variable Items

1. How many credits have you completed to date? _____

2. What is your age in years as of your last birthday?_____

3. Do you participate in organized collegiate athletics as a student athlete?
Yes_____
No_____

4. Are you a member of a college fraternity?
Yes_____
No_____

5. How would you best describe the amount of your sexual experience, compared to others your age? (Please place a mark on the line to indicate your response).

_____

No Experience   Very Experienced

Index